ASKING
FOR THE
ANCIENT
PATH

Walking in genuine relationship with your God

BY JEFF S. BARON

ASKING FOR THE ANCIENT PATH

ISBN: 978-0-615-29875-7

Library of Congress Catalog Number:
2009910522

Edited by Randy Ferguson and Joe Ford

Remnant Ministries Inc.
P.O. Box 5306
Longview, TX 75608
www.simplyreal.org

Printed in the United States by Morris Publishing®
3212 East Highway 30
Kearney, NE 68847
1-800-650-7888

This book is dedicated to the Exception.
May the truth found within these pages help you
to hear, trust, and obey God with all your heart.

TABLE OF CONTENTS

Author's note:

Each chapter of this book builds upon the other. Therefore, in order to benefit from the information within, it is highly recommended that the book be read starting at the preface. Since study and contemplation are anticipated, the Scripture references are printed within the body of the text to allow the reader to follow along with an open Bible.

FOREWORD

As I write this foreword, I realize there are some things you should know about the author. I have had the unique opportunity to experience being a part of his family. I have lived in his home, shared his food, laughed at his jokes, and enjoyed his friendship. The truths written within this book are the very expressions of his heart – a heart that has been disciplined and shaped by the grace of God and not men. I mean that to be no exaggeration of the truth – I have carefully observed a life completely given to God and set apart for the will of God. If you were to ask Jeff to sum up what he believes, he would likely tell you to repent, find God though it costs you everything, love Him with all your heart, with all your soul, with all your mind, and with all your strength, and die well.

Now, I don't write these things to flatter a friend or to bolster his image in your eyes. I write them to make a point. What is boldly professed in this book is not some ideal written merely to challenge you or to inspire you to recommit your life to God. It is written to point you to a very real relationship with the Living God who actually changes men. Jeff speaks of a lifestyle of following God with everything you know, a lifestyle in which you don't continue to live in sin anymore. God delivers men – truly – and the evidence of that is seen in the life.

It is because God truly delivers that this flame must be passed to the next generation. There is no reason why those who long to follow God should have to grope along in the dark, having to rediscover what has been lost. God wants to raise up real men and women of God – the True Church – to be a beacon of light for others who want to follow in a real way. Everything in a true Christian – their words *and* their actions – should reflect that God is real and intimately involved in the lives of those who belong to Him.

This book should be studied and pondered – aiding your pursuit of God. The truth should penetrate the heart and sink deep to the point of finding Him. It may be easy to skim over certain concepts or agree superficially with the parts that suit you, but that is not the purpose for which the book was written. In fact, the more challenging and costly the truth, the easier it can be to dishonestly dismiss or argue what is unpleasant to you. But will you weigh honestly what is presented to you? Will you pursue the truth when you are challenged? If so, this book will be of great benefit in helping you find God.

I find it important to note that this is not the type of book you read once and put on the bookshelf, but one that you will want to read again. When you read it through a second time, you will find that there is much more to be gleaned. It is common to find that, in teaching these concepts, many struggle to catch the truth the first time they hear it. In fact, several statements have come up so often that I will include some of them here:

"Oh, you mean I must give God *everything*."

"I must die to *that* too? I didn't realize when you said it would be costly, that you meant it would be *this* costly."

"That's what you mean by being honest with God – I must be honest with God about *every* motive?"

"Wow, I thought I understood – I thought I was doing better – I realize now I don't know *anything* apart from God – I *am* wicked."

The point is that as you read this book, it will challenge you to go deeper and point you to God. If you will find God and let Him change you, then you will discover even more.

Asking for the Ancient Path is a book that should be read with an open heart, a searching eye, and an appetite for truth. The individual with a willing heart will hunger for truth, even when that truth is hard to swallow. I challenge you to approach this book with a heart that longs for more. Cry out to God and search for Him as you read. As easy as it may be to read through quickly – don't. Meditate upon the things said, and test them for truth and substance. Let them disturb you where you're complacent. Then, carefully apply them to your heart, letting them change you. Your search for God should end in you actually finding God, even though it costs you everything you know.

"Wisdom is supreme; therefore get wisdom.
Though it cost all you have, get understanding."
Proverbs 4:7 (NIV)

Joe Ford

PREFACE

Christianity. It is considered to be the greatest of all religions. But in reality, true Christianity is not a religion at all, it is a relationship. It is a relationship with God through Jesus Christ. But, what is accepted by this generation as 'relationship' is a far cry from what New Testament believers accepted. Of course, the fundamental beliefs of Christianity remain the same. They consist of: Jesus' virgin birth (He was God in the flesh), His sinless life, His death upon a cross as a sacrifice for sin, His resurrection from the dead, His ascension into heaven, and His promised second coming. But, accepting these beliefs is in no way having salvation in Jesus. Neither does *claiming* a relationship with Jesus in any way actually mean *owning* a relationship with Jesus. And yet the existence of such counterfeit faith illustrates that there is a severe crisis in Christianity today, a crisis in how individuals are taught to *become* Christian.

Over two thousand years of religious contamination have altered what is generally accepted as 'salvation.' What was once an authentic encounter with God has become a simulated imitation. In the first century, Christians required a seeker to give a genuine confession demonstrated by a true repentance. This repentance was verified by a changed heart and a delivered life. Today, except in rare occasions, becoming a Christian has become a watered down experience of accepting a mental acknowledgement of Jesus, agreeing with the basic doctrinal concepts of Christianity, and praying a 'sincere' sinner's prayer. Although this is the common practice and has become acceptable throughout Christendom, it does not require actual deliverance from the practice of daily sin.

It is possible, however, to personally experience a relationship with God that is genuine and spiritual, rather than hypocritical and carnal. In order to do so, God must be found. It is to this end that this generation must explore the hidden truths found on God's ancient path, and learn what it means to walk with Him there.

INTRODUCTION

Who are you? Scattered among the millions of people in each generation are those few individuals whose hearts are . . . different. Individuals who when compared to the rest of the world stand out as unique. Now, not unique in that they are more attractive, more intelligent, or more gifted in areas valued by society. As a matter of fact, the opposite quite often is true. No, they are different in that they have a knowing deep in their hearts that there is more. They have a spiritual longing to hear that which is not heard, to see that which is not seen, and to know a truth that is seemingly unknowable.

These few, though clearly not perfect, strive to be changed; though they are not complete, they desire to be made whole; and though they exist in everyday life, they are drawn to live in such a manner as to be in contrast to that very life. They are an anomaly in this world. They are the Exception. When the world shifts its norm based solely on the selfishness of the day, and when popular opinion bullies and shoves society for its own wicked pleasure, those who are the Exception resist that selfish push – be it political, social, or religious. Especially when it is religious.

So the question begs an answer: Who are *you*? Are you the Exception? Are you a soul that is willing to seek deeper than those around you? Are you willing to peer behind the wizard's curtain and expose the charade for what it really is? Most will not choose this path. Most people will never risk losing their status, reputation, or acceptance by this world for the sake of such a truth. Those who are the Exception, however, will. If this is you, welcome. If not, it is my sincere hope that you will be by the end of this book.

I invite you to join me now, to look intently at those things the world fears to see, and to ponder a truth the religious will vehemently suppress. If you have ears to hear and eyes to see, I believe you will come to understand that which empowers the Exception to shake the very gates of hell.

JB

First, speak to God. Then let God speak to you. Let Him instruct you in His precepts. Let Him direct you.

Cyprian

His work begins in you by your wanting to turn away from your old life.

Fenelon

Going part way – is the same as not going at all.

Scott Gusa

All that self-denial can say is: 'He leads the way, keep close to Him.'

Dietrich Bonhoeffer

Chapter

1

THE ANCIENT PATH
(The Road Less Traveled)

"Thus says the Lord: Stand by the ways and see and ask for the ancient paths, where the good way is, and walk in it; and you will find rest for your souls."
Jeremiah 6:16

At first everything is out of focus . . . then the camera slowly pans up through a dense jungle to the unmistakable silhouette of a lean, rugged character standing alone with his thoughts. He removes his weathered hat to wipe his brow as he contemplates the next move of his adventure. Thus enters our typical Hollywood hero. You can tell by how he is dressed that he cares little for how he is perceived. His fashion sense speaks more to the practicality of his mission than to a concern for the style of the day. He is driven to the point of going it alone and suffering any and all consequences as a result of his pursuit. He is considered stubborn by his friends and fanatical by his contemporaries. Of what possible use is it to go tromping through uncharted territory risking your life, not to mention your reputation, to find something that most people say doesn't even exist?! What a waste of time. What a waste of money. What a waste of potential. And all on a venture that is nothing more than a pointless pipe dream. The quest, they say, is futile.

But our hero doesn't care about the personal cost or the taunts of the cynics. All he cares about is finding what has been missing for centuries, to rediscover the valuable object of old that the jungles of the world have concealed. To unearth what the passage of time has lost is a find of genuine significance and to him worth every effort.

ලෙ଼ଯ⬥ଅ৫ଅ৫ල⬥ଯ⬥ଅ৫ଅ৫ලେଯ⬥ଅ৫ଅ৫ලେଯ⬥ଅ৫ଅ৫ලେଯ⬥ଅ৫ଅ৫ල⬥ଯ⬥

Time has neglected many important things of the past, the most significant being the true path to finding a genuine relationship with God. Few walk with God anymore as Adam did on that most ancient of paths: honest, open, naked before Him who sees all. Yet, much like our hero, there are spiritual adventurers willing to seek out this ancient pathway buried long ago. Hidden by years of religious wrangling from the reformation to the reclamation, the true nature of walking with an engaging, compassionate Creator has long been obscured to man. Although habitually ignored by the naïve and regularly distorted by well-meaning clergymen, this ancient path is not lost to God. The original concept He created from the foundation of the earth has never been secreted away from His sight. And in no way has He ceased to reveal that way to any man, woman, or child who is willing to seek Him out.

It is because of His desire to be united with us that God "reveals the profound and hidden things" (Daniel 2:22). Not those things that have the appearance of depth yet prove false under the pressure of examination, but rather those thoughts of His heart and mind that pierce us to the very core of our soul. These are life-altering expressions that have a weight and value that break apart all the superficial pretenses in a person's heart. One heart – truly changed – speaks judgment to every heart that stagnates. This is true to the point that those who reject God's advances will find that they have at best only a shallow expectation of ever knowing Him.

This possibility of rejecting God necessitates an inspired heart response, one that is "stirred by a noble theme" (Psalms 45:1). A noble heart is one that is moved by the thoughts of God and is willing to search out the honest truth, regardless of the sacrifice required. The people of Berea were considered "more noble-minded" because they received the word about Jesus with eagerness and then examined the Scripture to see if what they were told was true (Acts 17:11). Yes, there are many things in the world that stir the hearts of the masses, and will do so until the end of the age. But it is only those who choose to see deeper, who choose to develop a heart that pleases God, and who choose to be the Exception that will find what is deep and what is hidden. Only a willing heart chooses to gaze past the obvious; to glimpse past the apparent. All too often it is easier to reject a truth than it is to search it out. This was especially true in the story about the pseudo-sailor.

An authentic sailor, who smelled of fish, had recently left his sizeable ocean vessel to purchase much needed supplies and found himself several miles from shore at a quaint mountain valley township. After acquisition of the items he required, he started back to the port through downtown. There, inexplicably, was a full-grown man dressed in a sailor's suit jumping up and down in a mud puddle exclaiming, "I'm in the ocean! I'm in the ocean!"

Now not being the sort of man who can let irrational behavior go unchecked, the sailor stopped and asked, "You're in the what?"

"The ocean – and I'm a sailorman."

The very thought of this charlatan defacing his profession would normally drive the sailor to violence, but the situation was so pathetic he decided to try persuasion instead. "Sir, I live on the ocean. I know the ocean. You are not standing in the ocean." Simple enough he thought; only a complete fool would refute such evidence.

"Well, I'll have you know that this *IS* the ocean because my father said so, my father's father said so, and his father's father said so – and what would you know – you reek!"

So the sailor, who as previously discussed did smell of fish, thought that maybe a more factual explanation would work. "Sir, I told you that I *live* on the ocean. It is stocked full of millions of fish and far deeper than the mountains are tall. The ocean stretches for miles and miles in almost every direction as far as the eye can see. God created it wondrous in the calm evenings and terrifying during a storm. You are in a mud puddle. Shallow, small, and landlocked."

But the pseudo-sailor retorted, "And I told you that it *was* the ocean because behind me is the *School of Ocean Going Sailors* of which I and all my forefathers graduated from. It was founded on the goal of knowing all things ocean related. *It* says this *is* the ocean, and nothing you can say will change that."

The sailor had honestly tried to get his attention and sincerely attempted to reason with him. Having been unsuccessful, the sailor – smelling of fish – returned to his ship.

Was the pseudo-sailor sincere in his perception? Of course. Wasn't there proof that generation after generation of witnesses proclaimed that he was right? Sure. Was he wrong? Yes, he was wrong and fully immersed in the deception. No matter how factual or even heartrending the attempt to gain his soul, this counterfeit was so gripped by his folly that he rejected even the most obvious, unpleasant aroma of truth. Why? I can't tell you how many times I've contemplated the question. When the truth is laid out like a roadmap and lit up like a freeway sign – a deep-seated perception will skillfully betray the mind. Are average people like the pseudo-sailor a hopeless cause? No, God is more than able to get their attention, but they must choose to respond.

Thus says the Lord: Stand by the ways and see
and ask for the ancient paths, where the good way
is, and walk in it; and you will find rest for your
souls.

In the main verse for this book, Jeremiah 6:16, God was trying to get the people of Judah's attention. He was trying to get them to see a way to Him that had been forgotten – an ancient way. The path was apparently not popular among the people – religious and non-religious alike. There were many other spiritual routes available to travel and God's wasn't as new, improved, and accepted. The Hebrew word for 'ancient' indicates the path was concealed and veiled from sight.[1] That couldn't have helped a self-absorbed, self-indulgent society look God's way. Besides, they already had a church to go to and plenty of spiritual leaders saying their way *was* God's way.

Hence the need to hear the "thus says the Lord" part of Jeremiah 6:16. When seeking God it is always best to . . . *seek God*. It may be difficult to realize that seeking God will require effort on your part. You may even discover that the struggle is arduous. But never fear – there will always be a myriad of voices available to offer you a way out, to offer you an easier path. Everyone has a friend, a preacher, a favorite religious person who is ready to offer all sorts of faulty advice. "Surely they couldn't be wrong – after all – they love me." Well I love you too, and would prefer you be more noble-minded and "not believe every spirit, but test the spirits to see whether they are from God . . ." (1 John 4:1). And that's exactly what is at stake here. Is what you believe really *from* God? Or are you caught up in the several 'acceptable' religious beliefs of our day?

These multiple viewpoints seem innocent enough. But it's these ways of thinking that God is saying to stand and see. Every personal belief from cradle to grave is on the chopping block. Stand right in the middle of all the options laid before you, all the ways you could go – and see. Look long and hard. Stare intently at the path you are on and then intently toward what God is trying to show you. Can you see the truth regarding your walk? Can you see the new path God is revealing? Or are you so hell-bent on going to heaven, you miss the path altogether? The hardest thing for you to do is be honest. It's difficult to recognize the truth because it can be so painful. The pride of man doesn't want to admit that there is more, much less that he is wrong.

Our self-importance will try to convince us that there really is no ancient path. I mean, come on! If it actually existed, someone would be writing books about it☺.

Once you cross into the mindset that there is more, the next stride is to ask God for direction. Every good thing comes from the Father (James 1:17), and He clearly says the ancient path is 'the good way.' You will not be able to progress unless you solicit assistance from the only person who can help you. Even with the best instruction and finest teaching tools, you will never be able to fully understand without the aid of the Holy Spirit (1 Corinthians 2:14). All of the best intentions and rigorous self-denial will be unproductive without God's guidance. The good news is that God "longs to be gracious to you; He rises to show you compassion" (Isaiah 30:18 NIV). He is a good God and at this very moment personally interested in your state and actively laboring on your behalf.

God is willing and able to train you in the way you should go, but the choice to actually walk the path is yours. Obedience is part of the covenant. *Now*, you will be effectively walking *His* will, no longer your own. Thus the possibility of hardship is very likely if you continue to pursue this course to the journey's end. If the path you are on is effortless, undemanding, and painless – you can be sure you are slowly sauntering your way to hell. Let the screams begin – "But Jesus said His yoke is easy!" (Matthew 11:30). No, that is a terrible translation, and He never said that. What He did say was that His yoke was *chrestos*, meaning profitable, fit, and good for any use. [2] So, if the road is difficult, challenging, and severe – *and* you are spiritually profiting from it – the bricks beneath your feet are probably gold.

Once you have stood and seen the ancient path; once you have sought God's assistance; and once you have been obedient to apply the path to your life – you will discover what it means to have rest. This is far more than a plastic, fuzzy, 'feel good' moment that removes a sense of guilt off your shoulders. It is also more than a self-justification that you are better than all those other people around you. Can't you see how unrestful it is to have to constantly convince yourself you're okay? That is no rest at all. When you are at rest you will cease to labor on your own. That means all attempts to save yourself will cease. All efforts to look good in your own eyes will end. There will be no need to plead your case to others, create some sort of self-value, or do something – anything – religious to feel different. You will be right with God, and you will actually *be* different. You will be at rest.

To condense this entire process into one word is easy . . . repent. Now repentance has gotten a pretty bad rap from all the Hollywood scenes of half-crazed want-to-be prophets carrying their placards up and down the sidewalk screaming, "Repent for the end of the world is near!" Then there is the fact that most churches today have conveniently changed the meaning of repentance to mean feeling sincerely sorry. I regret to inform you that a person can be sincere and yet be sincerely wrong. Repentance is much more than either of those. The definition of the word repent is "to change the mind."[3] Feeling sorry that you have sinned does not mean that you have changed; wanting to do better does not mean that you have changed; and wanting to avoid the punishment of hell does not mean that you have changed. Sadly these are nothing more than religious deceptions we tell ourselves to help us sleep at night. In spite of this, you may claim to have heartfelt remorse. Well, so did Judas when he betrayed Jesus and killed himself (Matthew 27:3-5). You have only been changed when you have been *changed*. Anything else is only a shallow attempt at repentance. When your mind has been altered, you don't think the same way anymore. The things that were enticing before, no longer have any pull on you. Even the noble religious desires that you once placed so much value on dissolve away to where only God remains. Then you have repented. Then you have found and are honestly walking on the ancient path.

From this basic primer, I hope to expand your awareness of God's ancient path. In the following chapters we will discuss a variety of issues, break down several concepts, and dispel numerous false theories. As we do so, remember that no matter how diligently you might study – you are desperately dependant on the Father to give you understanding and to grant you repentance (II Timothy 2:25). So let us walk together a short distance down the path, and see if the hidden things of God stir your heart as they do mine.

> *Two roads converged in the woods – I took the one less traveled by and it has made all the difference.*
>
> *Robert Frost*

Application Summary

There is a path to find God and to end your separation from Him. It is the way God originally determined for a man to find Him, and it is still available for you today. Although the road has been hidden by generations of good and evil intentions, God in His compassion wants to reveal it to you if you desire Him. He will guide you to see the truth of your life, and free you to perceive a better way. If you will choose this path, God will change you dramatically. The façade of the world will be exposed, and the pretense of religion will fade away. He will grant a true rest for your soul as you find the willingness to resign your self-importance; He will grant you a real respite to your heart as you turn from your own path; and He will give you a legitimate deliverance in your life as you reject your own attempts to deliver yourself.

Challenging Your Perception

1. Are you able to stand back and see that God's true way has been concealed by years of religious neglect?

2. Do you find, like the pseudo-sailor, that you have settled for a form of religion that is based on the compromised teachings of past generations?

3. Are you willing to let your heart be stirred by the reality of this more noble way and choose to respond in honest repentance?

Endnotes

1. James Strong, LL.D., S.T.D., *The New Strong's Exhaustive Concordance of the Bible*, Dictionary of the Hebrew Bible, copyright 1990 by Thomas Nelson Publishers, page 86, Hebrew #5769, *o-lawm,* page 89, Hebrew #5956, root *aw-lam.*
2. Spiros Zodhiates, TH.D., *The Complete Word Study Dictionary New Testament*, D/B/A AMG Publishers, copyright 1992 by Spiros Zodhiates and AMG International Inc. Zodhiates, page 1482, Greek #5543, *chreste.*
3. Ibid., page 969, Greek #3340, *metanoeo.*

Their preconceived perceptions caused them to disbelieve. If a man learns without preconceived ideas, he has ears to hear the truth.

Clement

Nothing mixed with truth results in truth.

Scott Gusa

Counterfeit the truth, and you forfeit reality.

Joe Ford

We never compromise out of ignorance, only out of knowledge.

Arthur Wallis

Chapter
2

A SINGULAR PERCEPTION
(No … You Don't Know)

*"The eye is the lamp of the body; so if your eye is clear, your whole body will
be full of light. But if your eye is bad, your whole body will be full of darkness.
If then the light that is in you is darkness, how great is that darkness."*
Matthew 6:22-23

We rejoin our hero as he has traversed through an almost
impenetrable jungle to his destination. What looks like any
typical rain forest to you and me – is so much more to the well-
trained eye. Efficiently disguised by years of vine growth, our
hero spies the entrance to a dimly lit cavern. As he cautiously
approaches the primeval cavity, the entire countryside goes silent
except his faithful steed, which snorts its displeasure. He enters
nonetheless. Letting his eyes adjust to the strange new
environment, what appears to be an ancient tribal king's burial
chamber starts to become visible. To the right, centuries-old
stalactites drip some unknown, murky liquid into hot, smoldering
fissures; to the left, more than one rotting carcass to serve as a
warning to the next fortune-hunter that dares approach the lair.
One step – and the whishing sound of a dozen flying poisonous

arrows triggers an instinctive dive forward. He performs a swift acrobatic flip and summersault that would make any gymnast proud. He spins and stands up no more than one inch from the edge of a bottomless pit. Was this almost the demise of our champion? Nah, he saw it coming the whole time. He's a hero.

ಚಿಚಿಚಿಚಿಚಿಚಿಚಿಚಿಚಿಚಿಚಿಚಿಚಿಚಿಚಿಚಿಚಿಚಿ

Does our hero falter? Does he fear for his life? No, undaunted he treads on. But why proceed in the face of such danger? Why risk so much for the plunder? Because he perceives value where others only see peril; he perceives danger where others only see the harmless props of some strange survival game. You see, it all depends on a person's perception.

So here's a little perception test I like to give when I meet new people or I am invited to speak somewhere. The answer a person gives, as much as the *way* a person answers, quite often exposes the contradictory nature of their belief system. I ask two simple questions:

Is God's grace unconditional?
Did Jesus come to bring peace on the earth?

The answer to both questions is no. Well, I've got your attention now. To verify the answer to the first question, Ephesians 2:8 says that it is by grace you are saved "*through* faith." Clearly the condition for grace is faith, and most people will be sheepish for never realizing the truth of it. (I'll go into more detail on this later in chapter 5). To substantiate the answer to the second question, you can go to Matthew 10:34-35 where Jesus Himself says:

> *Do not think that I came to bring peace on the*
> *earth; I did not come to bring peace, but a sword.*
> *For I came to set a man against his father and a*
> *daughter against her mother, and a daughter-in-*
> *law against her mother- in-law . . .*

Strangely, the answer 'no' is not what the average religious person would guess. As a matter of fact, most people will get down right disagreeable even after you reveal the answer in Scripture. Their predetermined perception of Jesus just won't let Him be that way. In the face of the obvious, they squirm to maintain not only their personal revision of the Bible, but strive to alter the very heart of our Savior.

Want a second chance? Here's another one:

> Do you love God with *ALL* your heart,
> with *ALL* your soul, and with *ALL* your mind?

Are you answering 'no' with a self-effacing, false humility that is supposed to gain you some kind of approval? It won't work. If the reply is not 'yes,' let me be the first to tell you that you will not inherit eternal life unless that changes. In Luke 10:25-28, a lawyer asked Jesus what must be done to inherit eternal life. Jesus asked him what he perceived the Scriptures to say. The man answered:

> *You shall love the Lord your God with all your*
> *heart, and with all your soul, and with all your*
> *strength, and with all your mind.*

Jesus told him that he was correct. He then told the lawyer, "Do this and you will live." The fact is if you don't love God with *ALL*, you'll have a hard time convincing Him you love Him *at all.* And yet many religious people will still justify themselves as they disagree with this verse. What does it say when professing 'Christians' allow their perceptions to continually challenge the Living God? What does it speak of the supposed relationship they so solemnly declare to embrace? What it reveals is that their heart and their perception are desperately askew. It reveals the reality that they are upside down.

If someone strolled up to you and promptly proclaimed that you were in fact upside down, are you the kind of person who would raise your hands to see if you could touch the ground? Or are you the sort who would reach up in defiance, seize two fistfuls of turf and boldly proclaim that you hold nothing in your grasp but air? Again with the predetermined perceptions! This becomes the very crux of the issue at hand.

At the root of every human heart lies the sinful desire to protect the self within. That defense manifests in such a broad variety of methods. From the polite, quiet difference of opinion to a full-blown conflict with rage, offense, and retribution. In truth, to perceive one's self honestly without resistance is paramount to finding God. You need to know where you are before you can find the directions to where you want to be. If you are unable to admit this reality, you are in a serious spiritual predicament. Maybe a quick story will help illustrate this concern.

A chef was talking with a young salesman at a restaurant supply store and happened to mention Jell-O® in their conversation. The salesman declared that he loved Jell-O® because it was so creamy. The chef stuttered a touch and pointed out that Jell-O® wasn't creamy; it was made with water and gelatin – kind of semi-opaque depending on the color. The salesman, much to the chef's surprise, then agreed and said that Jell-O® probably *had to be* to cover the cake. The chef puzzled for a second and stated that the salesman must have been thinking of icing for cakes. The salesman, confident in his folly, pronounced that they would just have to agree to disagree. The chef, now more than a little annoyed, pointed out that an amiable disagreement would never change fact into fiction. Then pondering the salesman's foolishness, the chef reluctantly went his way.

No amount of convincing would persuade the young salesman. No amount of earnest discussion would benefit his comprehension. He was steadfast in his opinion because his perception had misled him. Since he was unaware of the flaw in his position, the facts of the case meant nothing to him. Ultimately, his own understanding held sway over his ability to reason truthfully.

Several years ago I was visited by a hearty, eager young man named Mike. Now Mike was full of vigor and wit and had come to my house to 'find God.' He made it abundantly clear that he wanted to be a warrior for Christ in the worst way. And though I could appreciate such enthusiasm, there was a problem, a 'glitch' in his disposition if you will. To be sure, this is neither uncommon nor unfamiliar as all of us have multiple tendencies from birth that collaborate together to separate us from God. But God had caused a certain issue to surface during our discussion, and I learned a long time ago that if God brings it up, you deal with it. The conversation went something like this:

> Jeff: "Mike, I hear you, but you don't know what you are saying."
>
> Mike: "I know I don't know what I'm saying."
>
> Jeff: "No, I don't think you understand what I'm telling you . . . you don't *know* what you say you don't know."
>
> Mike: "I'm saying I don't know, that I don't know"
>
> Jeff: "See, that's what I'm trying to get across to you, that you don't *know* that you don't know."
>
> Mike: "Yeah, I know."
>
> Jeff: "No . . . you don't know."

Does this exchange sound strange? Well, it sure was when we had it. Yet the reality is quite common. Unless God has come into your life and changed you, changed the way you view . . . well, everything . . . you are seeing through diseased eyes. Mike was leaning solely on his own understanding (Proverbs 3:5), relying on his own perception of himself. That night God gave him a dream about his heart – he was standing in a vast nothingness, where God was showing him that he knew absolutely nothing. He had heard God. When he came back to me and said, "Now I know I don't know" – it was from God and not himself, it was true and not a fabrication, and it was life changing rather than life impairing. Once he truly perceived his condition, he was able to be changed.

Jesus said it was the sick that needed a doctor, not those who claim to be healthy (Matthew 9:12). And as long as you are preoccupied diagnosing and healing yourself, you won't need the Great Physician either. If a spiritually blind person claims to see, then God will hold that person accountable, and he will remain in his sin (John 9:39-41). When you 'already know' something, there is little room to hear the truth if you don't. What will happen when God speaks a truth to you, but you 'already know'? Like the Pharisees of old, you will have "no room" for His word (John 8:37). Realize that the prudent person gives honest thought to his ways, but a foolish person will wallow in his self-made deception (Proverbs 14:8 NIV).

Now you may be of the school that asserts that God doesn't speak today anyway, much like those who believe God is nothing more than a watchmaker who wound up the world and has left it to its own devices. It's easy for a blind man to believe there is no light or a deaf man to deny the existence of sound. So a person rejecting the advances of God will naturally not perceive them. In the story of Job, only one person receives no rebuke, Elihu. In his wisdom he makes a great point saying, "For God does speak – now one way, now another – though man may not perceive it" (Job 33:14 NIV). As long as God doesn't really speak, our flesh can do as it pleases. If there is no direction from Him, we presume there is no accountability for us. So, we choose a belief system early in life of a make believe deity that doesn't really speak. We create a weak-willed semi-god who is so gullible, naïve, and emotionally messed up that all He wants is for everyone to just get along. The truth is He does speak, but you need to choose to perceive it.

But will you? Will you choose to hear and perceive truth differently than you do now? The Greek word for 'truth' is defined as the "unveiled reality."[1] Everything God sees is uncovered. This is the honesty of all things unveiled for what they really are. For instance: If the motive of a person's heart seems to be pure – and it is – the truth reveals it to be so;

however, if the motive of a person's heart only appears pure –
but it is not – the façade is exposed and every shroud that
conceals it is shredded. No more hidden agendas, no more false
pretenses, no more part-time Christianity. Everything becomes
unveiled. The truth is known.

    This is not a notion that most worldly, or religious
people, want to entertain. It is much easier to live a life of self-
deception filled with polite excuse and courteous compromise.
But the ancient path is not effortlessly observed, much less
traveled. To embrace your own man-made reality and cling to
your own self-taught perception is a great deal like being
infected with a cancer of self that must be removed. You will
have to lose parts of yourself, parts that feel right to you – that
make you who you are. The many perceptions that you own
about God and the gospel may have to be released. But no one
ever said changing perceptions would be painless. The good
news is that God desires to heal you and change who you are to
the point that you will see the ailment for what it really is. With
the disease gone, you will see as God sees. With that said, let's
break down the main verse of this chapter, Matthew 6:22-23:

The eye is the lamp of the body . . .

    The first point of interest is that the Greek definition of
the root word for 'eye' is: to see, to perceive with the eyes. Now
this implies not only the mere act of seeing but also the actual
perception of what one sees.[2] This 'eye' is your personal
viewpoint of the universe – influenced by your family, friends,
experience and culture. It's how you choose to see things. It does
not infer that you see correctly or incorrectly, just that you
comprehend everything *your way*. Thus your eye, or the way you
perceive – good or bad – is the light you walk by. To what extent
this illumination enlightens you is not for certain. So therefore,
the question of accuracy involving the perception of ourselves,
God, and the world will become our central point of concern.

> *. . . so if your eye is clear, your whole body will be*
> *full of light.*

If the eye of your perception is 'clear' or single, it means that you are not seeing double as when diseased.[3] Understand that there is one truth, only one reality. It is God's truth, God's reality. Now, when you were born into this reality, you were infected with self and the disease of sin. Therefore, the way you see things is *not* clear – it is infected with *you*. The truth as God created it is now mixed with the truth as you recreate it. This self-made perception increases with every conversation and experience. The fact is that your double-vision *cannot* see clearly. Until God changes the way you see, you will continue to perceive and hold opinions based on your own chosen understanding. If, however, your perception is altered by God, you will see everything around you one way – God's way. You will see God's reality plainly. This singular perception will be clear, single, and healthy.

The Greek scholar Spiros Zodhiates explains the word 'clear' this way: "When the eye accomplishes its purpose of seeing things as they are, then it is *haplous*, single, healthy, perfect."[4] So if your perception sees things *as they really are*, then the way you perceive is accurate. Your eye then comprehends honestly, and your whole body is full of light. It is able to see the entire world – just as it is. Its viewpoint of God is true, and the perception of self is not deficient of integrity, being liberated from the infection of an egocentric opinion. It sees as God sees. And because it is no longer tainted with the double-mindedness of man, its vision is not blurred; on the contrary, it will have a focused singular perception in all things. Absent is the apprehension that something may be added to or taken away from the truth that is being seen. Now, with this type of enlightenment, a person can expect a dependable discernment without fear of self-contamination. Therefore, a clear, single eye refuses to make a situation complex just to win an argument; it does not shuffle a truth just to justify itself; and it will never try to shift a reality just to sleep better at night. The value of seeing things 'as they really are' is just too precious; the importance of illumination too dear.

> *But if your eye is bad, your whole body will be full*
> *of darkness. If then the light in you is darkness,*
> *how great is that darkness.*

If however, the eye of your perception is bad, the verse implies that all possibility of enlightenment disappears. The basic Greek definition for 'bad' is evil. It comes from the root word to labor – to labor with all the strength of man.[5] So Jesus makes the point that a diseased perception is infected with the self-labor of man. This type of insight does not find its source in God, but rather is artificially created from the efforts of the individual. Although it may have a form of worldly wisdom, moral ideology, and even sound biblical principle – it is contaminated with ego and self-interest. When the arm of man flexes, it brings its power to bear purely for its own end.

This disease of man-made duplicity has become an acceptable hypocrisy. An individual may insist that his intention is completely innocent, his purpose unimpeachable; yet with very little inspection, the angle of his veiled, ulterior motive becomes obvious. Far too many professing 'believers' are darkened and deceived by their own sight – fully convinced that their blindness is light.

In Matthew 5:30, Jesus makes a very bold – seemingly outrageous – remark. He states that, "If your right *hand* makes you stumble, cut it off and throw it from you." Now, throughout the Scripture it is notable that when the right hand of man is mentioned, it is referring to the strength of man – that arm of man which he depends upon. So, the point is that if you are depending on your own arm of the flesh, it is clear that you are not trusting on God's strength. When the inevitable happens and your dependence on your own ability causes you to stumble, the Lord's solution is to cast off the sinful flesh because it will cause "your whole body to go into hell."

This stumbling is far more than a mere stagger or slip of the foot, it is to *skandalizo*. From the root *skandalon*, often translated offense, it is the bait set on a trigger of a trap meant to entice and ultimately ensnare an animal. The Greek definition goes further to involve the conduct of the person so trapped, denoting an enticement to conduct which leads to ruin.[6] So the assertion Jesus is making is not some grotesque effort of self-mutilation but rather an attempt to deliver you – from you.

Come to the point of realization that your own labor, your chosen conduct of relying on your own understanding, is deceiving and ensnaring your soul. Then you will be able to understand that you do not have to be persuaded by your flesh anymore. You can refuse to 'take the bait' that leads to ruin by ceasing your own effort – even your well-meaning religious behavior that only seeks to justify the self – and thereby turn more deeply in heart toward God.

The verse found just before this one (29) states, "If your right *eye* makes you stumble, tear it out and throw it from you." The word for eye once again is the idea of how you perceive, and when combined with the concept of your 'right' eye and *skandalon* – the picture Jesus is painting for us becomes much more transparent. If your strong eye – or preferred perception – leads you to a faulty understanding, it will cause your ruin. To continue to hold to a viewpoint for whatever reason – stubbornness, ego, or any other motive ultimately rooted in the self – is to remain blinded to the light that is just beyond your darkened understanding. Pluck out that contaminated, ensnaring understanding and cast it far from you. Choose rather the perception that God is attempting to give you.

Another verse that will aid our discussion is what Jesus said in John 16:16 (NIV). Depending on the translation, it reads like this:

> *In a little while you will see me no more, and then*
> *after a little while you will see me.*

Does this Scripture sound confusing? Or is there more to the verse than meets the eye hidden just below the surface? The first word for 'see' is *theoreo*, to look with interest and for a purpose.[7] This word holds the meaning to be a spectator.[8] Whereas the second word for 'see' is *optanomai*, meaning to actually perceive what one sees.[9] So what Jesus was really saying wasn't nearly so confusing after all. He said that in a little while you will no longer just be an interested spectator; soon you will actually perceive me. Imagine this: actually perceiving the Savior as He really is. No longer having to be confused by apparent riddles; no longer having to just be a spectator of God; no longer seeing double through the eyes of man. How the people of this world could use this today! To own a single, pure perception of the God that sees all things clearly. Now that will change a person profoundly.

This raises the query: Do you have a singular perception? I hope you didn't just impulsively answer 'yes.' This entire exercise is to get you to go to God for these types of answers. How do you know if you have a perception problem – if you have a problem in how you perceive in the first place? You can't know, unless God reveals to you the unveiled truth about yourself. So where do you choose to place your effort: striving to be justified and right in your own perception, or will you choose to make every effort to see clearly and be right in the sight of God?

The ancient path is calling out to us to see differently, to change the way we perceive. To travel this road we will need to see with God's perception and trust what he reveals. If we don't question our blindness, we will never get the answer of light. We all need our double vision to be corrected, and there is only one Physician who can cure us. And when we find Him, we will be.

Application Summary

Every person is born with a spiritual disease of the eyes. You see what you want to see, and how you want to see it. This causes your understanding to walk in darkness blinded to the unveiled reality. But here is an awakening, a time set by God to wake you up; to help you see the things you couldn't, or wouldn't, see before. To follow the ancient path is to open your eyes and choose to see yourself honestly. Not only that, but you will see friends, family, and the church in a light never seen before. The entire revelation can be quite painful. You can choose to pretend that there is no 'more' and play a game by refusing to acknowledge reality. But if you will choose to hear God and receive the cure from Him – you can know the truth and have a clear, singular perception.

Challenging Your Perception

1. Are you able to perceive the reality that God is speaking to you? When God's voice challenges your perception, are you willing to see where you are upside down?

2. Do you find your perception is infected with your own understanding? Can you see how this has become an acceptable hypocrisy in your life?

3. Will you choose to hear and perceive truth differently than you do now? Are you willing to throw out your bad perceptions to gain a clear, singular understanding of God?

Endnotes

1.   Spiros Zodhiates, TH.D., *The Complete Word Study Dictionary New Testament*, D/B/A AMG Publishers, copyright 1992 by Spiros Zodhiates and AMG International Inc., page 120, Greek #225, *aletheia*.
2.   Ibid., page 1081, Greek #3788, *ophthalmos*, page 1052, Greek #3700, root *optanomai*.
3.   Ibid., page 214, Greek #573, *haplous*.
4.   Ibid.

5. Ibid., page 1198, Greek #4190, *poneros*, page 1199, Greek #4192, root *ponos*.

6. Ibid., page 1292, Greek #4624, *skandalizo*; Greek #4625, *skandalon*.

7. Ibid., page 733, Greek #2334, *theoreo*.

8. James Strong, LL.D., S.T.D., *The New Strong's Exhaustive Concordance of the Bible*, Dictionary of the Greek Testament, copyright 1990 by Thomas Nelson Publishers, page 36, Greek #2334, *theoreo*.

9. Ibid., page 1052, Greek #3700, *optanomai*.

It's not about bringing God into my world; it's all about bringing me into God's world.

Robert Marta

We should allow the name of Jesus to be engraved deeply on the heart, written there by the finger of God Himself in everlasting characters.

William Wilberforce

God makes Himself known to those who, after doing all that their powers will allow, confess that they need help from Him.

Origen

Relationship, relationship, relationship.

Scott Gusa

Chapter

3

THE LIVING GOD

(Finding God in This Present Moment)

". . . for he who comes to God must believe that He exists and that He rewards those who earnestly seek Him."
Hebrews 11:6 NIV

"I found it! I knew I'd find it!" the hero exclaims in a triumphant voice. His ecstatic words echo off the walls, reverberating back and forth around the immense cavern. There in front of him, amid the stench of a putrid fog, he can at last behold his long, sought after trophy. Carefully perched upon a carved stone pedestal and surrounded by fire is the unmistakable, crimson glow of the priceless Giant Ruby. Finally, after all the struggle, after all the pain, after all the ridicule – he is exonerated. He has managed to acquire that which so many back home whispered to be hopeless. What the cynics said was impossible, he found to be possible; what the naysayers said was unachievable, he concluded to be achievable; and what the pessimists said was unattainable, he proved beyond the shadow of a doubt to be attainable. Because of grit and tenacity, he has obtained what few will ever dream of finding in their lifetimes.

Was it hard? Of course it was. Was it dangerous? Absolutely. Was it worth losing everything he had ever come to love and hold dear in his life? For certain – and then some.

CRORCRORCRORCRORCRORCRORCRORCRO

To find the impossible staggers the mind – the base understanding of mankind flails out of control with the thought of possessing the priceless. And God is beyond priceless. The reality that a mere, mortal human being can intimately know the Living God who created him and experience a genuinely close relationship is the greatest news bulletin in all of history. Why then isn't this passionately broadcast by the entire world? Simply because, to choose the path that leads to God is to deny every other pathway that leads to self-interest, self-indulgence, and self-importance.

The haughtiness of the human race is ever ready to dissuade the curious back to a road less radical. "There is no God," says the person who looks more like a harmless librarian than a monstrous Satanist nefariously plotting to steal your soul. "You've already found Him," declares the preacher who has become so self-convinced of his own watered down excuse for 'Christianity' that in his misery he manipulates your spirit to join his. These are the talons that steal among the shadows longing to drag one more soul into blindness. To hearken to this intoxicating melody is the promise of a lifetime stumbling in the darkness.

God, however, is like a light illuminating in the middle of the pitch black universe. As He shines, the darkness loses what makes it dark. Reality is clearly seen for the plain truth that it is – with no shadow or shade. Of course the darkness hates the light, because the dark thrives on *hiding* reality. The darkness abhors the light because it can no longer hold sway over the souls of men; it can no longer blind their eyes to what is true. The Spirit of God is honest and real, and people with perceptive hearts gather to Him. These enlightened ones are now absent from the galaxy of gullible inhabitants that foolishly thrash about and bump into the unseen. Somebody walked in and turned on the light.

The fact is . . . God *wants* to be found. He is and always has been revealing Himself. He is neither vague in His revelation nor ambiguous about His will. God is even revealing Himself to you right this very minute. Yes, He is, don't argue☺. Romans 1:19-20 says that what is known about God is being made evident to you through creation. You know – the tree outside your house, the air you're breathing, even the skin on your face is His testimony to you. The Scripture says His attributes, power, and divine nature have been *clearly seen*. The Bible goes so far as to say that since God has been made evident to you – you have no excuse. This means that deep down inside – past every pretense, deception, and little white lie – you know the truth. Maybe it is creatively concealed by inspired intellect or excessive emotion. Maybe it is deeply buried under years of friendly influence or malicious manipulation. Or maybe it is just thinly passed over by basic root selfishness. But it's there. Your heart of hearts knows that God is speaking. Deep down inside of all that you hold dear – you see Him. You know that He exists.

But this truth of God is often concealed deep in the heart or altered by false perceptions in order to re-create Him as less than who He really is. It should be discussed that the Eternal Lord is more than just a baby Jesus in a manger or an historical bearded prophet in a robe and sandals. He is more than the clichéd 'big buddy upstairs' or the stereotypical, deeply voiced, giant old guy on a throne. God is not ordinary, weak, or common. Upon honest inspection, the opposite is true – God is quite uncommon. Though He has reached out to ordinary man, He is anything but ordinary.

For my thoughts are not your thoughts, neither
are your ways my ways, declares the Lord. As the
heavens are higher than the earth, so are my ways
higher than your ways and my thoughts than your
thoughts.
(Isaiah 55:8-9)

The unveiled reality is – that God *is*. God has even made this statement Himself to Moses when he told him – I AM (Exodus 3:14). He repeated the declaration when He walked among men as Jesus, and told the Pharisees, "Before Abraham was born, I AM" (John 8:58). God has also spoken to every person ever born through the metaphor of the world surrounding them that the universe has a Creator. And some even accept it as true.

> *. . . for he who comes to God must believe that He*
> *exists and that He rewards those who earnestly*
> *seek Him.*

Although it's great for God to be real in someone else's life, to personally accept the reality of God yourself is a necessary progression. This chapter's central verse, Hebrews 11:6, not only affirms the existence of the Father but that we can draw near to Him. God is authentic, definite, and actual. He is here – approachable, touchable, and knowable. All of the best intellectual and emotional arguments that the world could impose will never change that reality. God lives.

With the existence of God recognized, the verse puts the onus to believe squarely on the shoulders of the seeker. To simply acknowledge He exists or to even wholeheartedly accept all the stories in the Bible is not enough. In order to honestly approach the Father, one must *believe* that He truly exists, that He is real. The condition to believe is an actual requirement to draw near to God in the first place. One of the more dramatic problems with the world, and more particularly the church world, is that the word 'believe' has come to mean nothing more than mere mental assent. Please understand that there is much more to believing than just giving a stark, rational consent or a heartfelt, emotional agreement. Intellectual awareness supported by deep-seated sincerity is not the act of believing. To believe is to *pisteuo*, to trust.[1]

Let's say you and a perfect stranger agree that your newborn baby is cute. You agree that babies are a gift from God.

And because of a bad personal experience, the stranger is even sincerely emotional about the need of constant care for children. Does that mean you would trust the stranger with your child? Would you leave on a vacation with your baby in the hands of that person for two weeks because you agree? Of course not – you don't know him nor trust him.

To know God you must genuinely trust. This is non-negotiable. Any pious act that imitates reliance on Him is quickly branded a counterfeit. Because God perceives the truth about your heart plainly, no hypocritical deed ever goes unnoticed. With His perfect eye searching the innermost parts of your being, any tainted actions serve only as proof of compromise. Do you dwell upon the earth knowing that a living and breathing God is watching your every movement, hearing your every thought? Or do you find that you only really 'believe' that when you're feeling and acting religious? Trust that is not genuinely honest – is no trust at all.

The next part of the main verse states that God rewards those who "earnestly seek" Him. To do this is to *ekzeteo*, to seek out – to search diligently for anything lost.[2] If you are only seeking half-heartedly, you are wasting your time. This too is non-negotiable. It is only those who desire to find God with *all* that is in their being who will be rewarded. As Jeremiah 29:13 says:

You will seek Me and find Me when you search
for Me with all your heart.

If God decrees the truth to be that to find Him you must seek with *all* your heart, then everything else is a lie. Yet for some reason, to presume that you can obtain salvation without seeking God with *all* your heart is a very common and widespread disease. This is a self-made, self-taught infection that spreads deception to the core of uninformed souls. To accept that lie in order to feel better about your eternal state generally means a lowering of the standards to justify your position. There is great reward in finding God, but no reward is given to those who modify God's requirements. You must seek with *ALL*.

This reward that God gives those who diligently seek should in no way be confused with the riches of this world. The rewards of God have merit and significance unlike the treasures of the earth that moth and rust destroy (Matthew 6:19). The overwhelming value of a deep relationship with the Father is substantially more precious than any amount of earthly silver or gold. And it is awarded to those who want God so bad it hurts. A broken and contrite heart will ache for God, longing for Him as the trivial activities of the day go by. To be free from self and given totally to God becomes the heart's cry. This type of intimate heart awareness stands in such stark contrast to well-meaning, religious motions. Dry, religious theology does not satisfy the spiritually hungry; exaggerated, mystical charismata will not quench the thirsty. To dispute otherwise is simply unperceptive.

Some would argue that there is usefulness in at least being around a religious atmosphere. Beware the lie of proximity. Just because a person is around God, it does not mean that it will make him close to God. Judas spent years in the actual physical presence of Jesus to no avail; multitudes of people ate the fish and the loaves yet never darkened the door of the upper room; and millions of people attend Sunday services around the world never choosing to change and find the Father intimately in the present moment. To esteem being close to the narrow gate, yet never entering in – is fatal, the very poison of religion. God gives no credence to the uncommitted. Should a person be praised for his proximity if there is no intimacy? No, his stubbornness should be reprimanded.

Discovering God personally is infinitely more honest than just finding religion. Religion consists of a wide variety of principles and traditions that have a very heartfelt sense of devotion to them. So much so, that the entire process can subsist quite well without the presence of God at all. It is relatively common in religious circles to meet people who claim to own a relationship with the Father, only to realize later that it is nothing more than a learned, religious response stemming from years of pious self-perception.

When a man follows a woman around under the false assumption that he has a relationship with her – it is called *stalking*. If you are following God around by going to church, Bible studies, and mission trips – yet have no genuine relationship – it is paramount to religious stalking. The difference, you would say, is that your devotion is deep and sincere – well, so would the stalker.

The old adage says 'birds of the feather flock together,' and it is never truer than in the world of religious stalkers. In fact, a religious person who boldly asserts a presumption of relationship with God will be quickly received among the shallow, while a genuine follower is rebuffed for attempting to expose hidden truth. But if seeking to find God in a deeper way is grounds for religious dismissal, the Exception is willing to pay that cost.

This 'deeper way' is a true relationship with the Father that extends to the very foundation of the heart. It is a profound knowledge of God, a confidence in Him that refuses to be swayed by any false pretense. An association this honest alters the very existence of a man. God, a living person, becomes the very center of everyday life, and all other unrealities vanish. This means that knowing God is neither imaginary, nor wishful thinking. No more make-believe Christianity; no more false forgiveness; no more religious games. Any and all false expectations invented to ease the conscience are discarded with contempt. The heart that once hid from the sight of a distant, angry judge now runs to the arms of an ever-present, loving father.

It is in this present moment that God is found. You cannot find Him yesterday; it is gone with all the opportunities afforded to it. You cannot find Him tomorrow; it is not here yet – with no guarantee that it ever will be. No, you must find Him today as the Scripture says – "now is the day of salvation" (II Corinthians 6:2). Though it cost you your belief system, find God. Though it cost you your family, find God. Though it cost you your reputation, your career, and everything you own – find God. Hold nothing in reserve – let every motive be laid bare before Him.

Now, seeking God in the moment is not truly seeking *God* if the motive is me. I will not find God if my ulterior motive is to get to go to heaven, nor will I find God if my objective is to avoid suffering in hell. These are selfish desires. Searching for God and His kingdom rule has nothing to do with sorting out the lodging and accommodations of the afterlife. He never said to seek a location with all the heart, soul, and mind. Therefore, my search for the Father shouldn't end by discovering *me*. If my intention is to be relieved from the condemnation and guilt of not living a godly life, the truth of my wicked intent will be found out. God will not be mocked. It doesn't make Him happy when you find what pleases 'you' – He is glad when you find what pleases Him.

To truly encounter the Father in the present moment is to experience Song of Solomon 4:9:

> *You have stolen my heart, my sister, my bride; you*
> *have stolen my heart with one glance of your eyes . . .*

The thought that with one glance toward God we could steal His heart is astonishing. The thought that God in all His greatness would be moved to such passion for *us*, is almost unbelievable. Yet, the prize of this kind of intimacy is given to those who seek His way and walk His path. Even King David pondered the benevolence of God when in Psalms 8:4 he asks, "What is man that you are mindful of Him?" Can you utter with any confidence an answer? To do so is folly. We are nothing; He is everything. But God in His goodness allows us to find Him – and then rewards us with His heart.

After finding the Father, hearing the clamor of the latest spiritual craze becomes nothing more than the propaganda of a conman's new 'guilt removal' snake oil. Why drink the poisonous illusion of an elixir meant to dull the senses when the legitimate medication is in the palm of your hand? Yet the wicked of the world will continually settle for the appearance of relationship rather than coming to terms with the deeply hidden disgrace that their plastic religion is a cheap imitation of the real thing.

You can rejoice to know, however, that finding God is not too difficult for you, not out of your reach (Deuteronomy 30:11). He is very near you; find Him. And when you find God in each breath of your life, it will be the greatest thing you've ever known. In His presence, there is no sin. In His presence, there is no self. In the presence of an awesome, loving God, everything fades away to reveal the truth – there is only God. There are few who will be willing to walk this narrow path to a relationship with God – and when they do, they will be rewarded.

Application Summery

God is real. He is not dead; He lives. And He is the light that will illuminate all of your reality. The value of knowing the Father staggers the mind. More than an historical figure or a make-believe fantasy, God can be found in the present moment, and He wants to be found – by you. If you will search for Him diligently with no pretense or posturing, you will be rewarded with a deep, intimate relationship. One glance from your eyes will set God's heart on fire. You will join those few who desire something more than religion and will find Him when you seek Him with all your heart. Once you have discovered true relationship with God in each moment, you will find everything else completely shallow in comparison. Finding God is not too difficult, not out of your reach. You *can* find God.

Challenging Your Perception

1. Are you able to realize how very real God is? If God is this real, how does that change the way you make your decisions, the

way you pray, and the way you follow God?

2. Upon close examination – do you actively trust God in the present moment? Do you have an intimate relationship with God, or do you justify yourself by saying you do?

3. What are you really seeking? Are you seeking to avoid the punishment of hell? Are you seeking the comfort of heaven? Or are you actually seeking *God*?

Endnotes

1. Spiros Zodhiates, TH.D., *The Complete Word Study Dictionary New Testament*, D/B/A AMG Publishers, copyright 1992 by Spiros Zodhiates and AMG International Inc., page 1160, Greek #4100, *pisteuo*.
2. Ibid., page 540, Greek #1567, *ekzeteo*.

To be a disciple means to be disciplined by the heart of God. Trust His influence of grace as it changes you. In this way, you will become His child.

Jeff Baron

[God] has never committed Himself to bless our plans. He prefers to bless what He Himself has initiated.

Arthur Wallis

The Bible directs us to pray for the influence of the Holy Spirit to enlighten our understanding, to dispel our prejudices, to purify our corrupt minds, and to renew us after the image of our heavenly Father.

William Wilberforce

Cheap grace is the preaching of forgiveness without requiring repentance . . .

Dietrich Bonhoeffer

Chapter 4

A GENUINE GRACE

(Much More than Mercy)

"For by grace you have been saved . . ."
Ephesians 2:8

Our triumphant hero now exits the dark jungle with his prized Giant Ruby securely stashed in the knapsack slung across his shoulder. He walks down the dusty road into an insignificant border town bustling with outdoor markets. He'll need a stable for his horse, some food for his stomach, and a bed for his tired and worn out body.

But wait, what's that low tone permeating through the alleys of the town? It comes and then it goes. This community is too poor to have any high-powered equipment around. Does anyone else hear it? No. There it is again. Maybe it's just the imagination of an over-worked mind. After all, it's been a long day. So, with a few dollars he rents a room and settles in for some well-deserved slumber. But within a few hours, strange dreams cause a restless sleep. The ever-increasing throb of some bizarre resonance finally startles the hero awake. A bright crimson glow now pulsates throughout the blackness of the room. Glancing across the flat, his eyes settle on the knapsack sitting on the floor in the corner. It appears that the eerie illumination originates there. Although it seems impossible, he is sure of it now – the Giant Ruby is calling to him.

Should he believe it? Should he even consider the fantastic probability? Or should he just forget the entire incident and unload the artifact at the nearest museum? If even his closest friends thought he was crazy before, they would say he is certifiable now. How could the reality of a speaking rock make sense to the scrutiny of a skeptical science community – when it doesn't even make sense to the person who claims to have heard it in the first place? It's not natural. It's not possible. And yet there it is, radiating – calling out to the man who discovered it after all these years.

ಲಚಿತಿ೧ಲಚಿತಿ೧ಲಚಿತಿ೧ಲಚಿತಿ೧ಲಚಿತಿ೧ಲಚಿತಿ

Coming to terms with the reality of a Living God that speaks can be just as challenging. So much so, that the predominant theory created by man is that God does not concern Himself with the details of our actions as long as we hold ourselves to some sort of moral code. Although these doctrinal inventions are formidable to the intellect of men, God is not daunted by such fabrications. He has purposed to reveal Himself in every aspect of our lives and thereby shape the very center of our being. He does this by grace.

The Greek word for grace is *charis*. It is defined as, "the divine influence upon the heart, and its reflection in the life."[1] This 'influence' of God also causes, affects, changes, and transforms a person.[2] As this definition is too long to continually use, I will use a working definition: Grace is God's changing influence. To better understand the extent of God's grace and the concept that it is a changing influence, let's look at Titus 2:11-12:

> *For the grace of God has appeared, bringing*
> *salvation to all men, instructing us to deny*
> *ungodliness and worldly desires and to live*
> *sensibly in the present age . . .*

First of all, the fact that grace is "instructing us" illustrates the reality that it is an active endeavor, a specific, engaging action aimed toward us for our change. Secondly, the Greek word for "instructing" originally meant to bring up and educate a child. This education was the activity of training a child and influencing his conscious will and action.[3] Consequently, when God shows us grace, He is actively instructing and influencing our lives to say no to this world. Thus through His changing grace, we are enabled to be free from the ungodliness and worldly desires that exist in our own hearts. This was His original intent of grace, and it has never changed.

To further illustrate this point, let's discuss what genuine grace *is not*. Grace is not mercy. Again I say . . . grace is *not* mercy. Mercy means to show compassion.[4] And though God is indeed compassionate in His grace influence toward us, grace is more than just compassion – more than just mercy. It can be said that mercy may be moved to compassionate action, but that action – unlike grace – does not require change. Thus if mercy were to illicit change, it would cease to be mercy and it would become the changing influence of grace.

Let's employ for example a commonly used phrase: I'll just show him grace. Suppose you are in a discussion with a friend and realize that he is wrong. Although his understanding is faulty and he needs to be told the truth, you don't want to lose a good relationship with him by disagreeing. So you decide to 'just show him grace.' Your intent is to show your friend compassionate mercy and forget the whole thing. The issue is allowed to fade away – thus keeping the relationship intact, as well as your friend's error. Now, did you notice that the word for grace used in this scenario is the exact opposite of its true meaning? Rather than grace being an influence of change in the friend, it was watered down to mean – don't influence change.

But if we use the accurate definition of grace in the story, it would make the account different altogether. You are in a discussion with your friend and realize he is wrong. Knowing his understanding is faulty, you choose to show him grace. You speak the truth to him attempting to influence a change in his understanding. Because your friend is now aware of the reality, he becomes accountable for the truth that has been graced into his life. And the choice whether or not to respond to that changing influence is his. You might be saying, "Wait a minute, if I 'grace' into his life this way – it may cause division." Yes, the changing influence of the unveiled reality of God is very divisive. Truth is a light that has a way of separating every true follower – every Exception – from the warped, shadowy perceptions of this world. Yet men in their wickedness love to alter that truth.

Many Biblical words like this have been twisted throughout Christendom to suit the convenience of men. As we have previously discussed, words such as repent and believe have been warped by this kind of fraud. And now we see that the true meaning of grace has been strangled by the doctrinal vines of men as well. To dumb down the original intent of the Father's heart in the area of grace is to cause irreparable harm to the truth. The false doctrine of grace as mercy damages everything from the basics of salvation to the depth of an intimate relationship with God.

For by grace you have been saved . . .

Ephesians 2:8, the main verse of this chapter, will aid greatly in substantiating my concern for this reality. It states, "For by grace you have been saved . . ." The condition for salvation is grace. This is a biblical fact. It is also a fact that God did *not* say that it is by mercy we are saved. No, it is by God's changing influence that men are delivered. Genuine grace *changes*. Again let me say, although God is definitively merciful in His choosing to show us this grace, grace is more – it is His active influence on us to be transformed.

This need to be transformed by God's influence is why Jesus said in John 6:44 that, "No man can come to Me, unless the Father who sent Me draws him." Verse 45 goes on to say that it is those who have heard *and* learned from the Father that come to

Jesus. So, as important as hearing the voice of God is, this proves it is just as important to actually learn what the Spirit of grace is teaching you. Thus, the reality is that no one can come to Jesus unless it has been granted by the Father (John 6:65), and God determines that based on your willingness to learn from Him. Know that God gives the ability to deny ungodliness only to those who respond to His influence. And it is only then that they can say, "we are saved through the grace of the Lord Jesus" (Acts 15:11).

There is a great deception that clouds the minds of those who have not let God influence them and completely deliver them from the day by day dominion of sin. It is the convincing ruse of acceptable compromise. When people claim to have given Jesus their lives but deep down inside they don't really love God with *all* their hearts, they tend to migrate to the lie that – though they are admittedly only half-hearted – somehow everything will be excused. But there is even a greater deception when these same people are fully convinced that God's mercy makes it all okay because they think the Bible says so. To counterfeit genuine grace as mercy is to fashion it into a damnable doctrine.

Most people believe that they don't have to really change. Too many people consider that the only changes required are the ones accepted by the socio-religious organization they visit on Sunday. And far too many people boldly boast of a supposed sincere change that God has made in them, while still being bound by bitterness, selfishness, and ego. The truth of their lives proves that they have wasted the opportunity of His influence and remain untransformed. When God's grace comes to you, you know it. When God graces you, you are changed. When God's changing influence becomes part of your life – you become the type of person you have only previously pretended to be.

When you realize that God wants to be found and is even influencing mankind to find Him, it makes you stop and wonder how the original definition for grace affects other verses. I would not be doing the concept of an influential, changing grace justice without examining at least a small number of these verses to help you perceive this lost aspect of God's ancient path. So, let's look at some.

In Acts 20:24, Paul is testifying about the "gospel of the grace of God." The word gospel originally meant 'the reward for good news' and later became just 'good news.'[5] Thus Paul is actually testifying to more than just the story of Jesus. He is giving witness to the reality that Jesus is the good news of the changing influence of God. That God sent His son to live and die as an example for us must become more than just a distant, vicarious experience. Christ was not just our substitute on the cross. He didn't die so we wouldn't have to. He died as an example to influence change in us, so that we would let go of this world and lay down our *own* lives and die to ourselves – just as He did. This is the good news: You don't have to stay the same anymore. God can change you if you will respond to His influence.

The fact is that you may choose to reject these advances of God. This can be seen in II Corinthians 6:1 where it is urged "to not receive the grace of God in vain." This makes it apparent that people who are being influenced by God can refuse to allow Him to change them. The word vain means empty and meaningless.[6] If God's original intent is to influence you to the point that you reflect His change in your heart, and yet you refuse that genuine change – it is vanity, it is meaningless. Many religious people will vainly go through the motions of changing everything from outward appearance to internal self-denial. Yet, if these are based on the influence of pious traditions or stereotypical, spiritual 'good ideas' – then the grace of God will have been subjugated by man's religion. I've always said that if the road to hell is paved with good intentions, then the rocks in that pavement are good ideas. These sincere, well-meaning notions are nothing more than man-made inventions that originate from self-value. Understand that there is no benefit to the influence of God unless you let *God* influence you. So, don't take the grace of God in vain.

The next point I'd like to make is that "God is opposed to the proud, but gives grace to the humble" (James 4:6). Again, this is very good news. It is God's desire to influence you to perceive and to act in accordance with the truth. Those who will humble themselves in response to His voice will continue to receive the engaging hand of God in their lives. But if you are arrogant and are under some sort of presumption of innocence – God will oppose you. Let me go further to say that if you are right at this moment proudly presuming upon some doctrinal stance that stands in disagreement to these truths – God opposes *you*. And that is *your* choice. Both arrogance and humility are choices. If you choose pride, God will not change you. But if you will choose to humble yourself, God will transform you.

You see, godless people "change the grace of our God into a license for immorality" (Jude 4 NIV). This is what happens in practice when grace becomes mercy. God's grace, which teaches us to say no to ungodliness, is selfishly altered to become an excuse to stay the same. Grace is not a spiritual get out of hell free card, nor is it your lucky train ticket to heaven. These types of deceptive doctrines distort the truth like the proverbial rose-colored glasses. The belief is that though we are really wicked and in sin, Jesus sees us through His blood and pretends we are holy. But Jesus does not just look at you through His blood, He cleanses you with it. God's intent is not to play make-believe with your soul. God influences us to be delivered from sin – and that means no more sin. You can actually become holy, not just act like it.

The most terrifying element for many is found in the latter part of Jude 4. The verse continues, saying that when these people change grace – they "deny Jesus Christ." I sure hope you just heard that. Maybe they change it because of wicked self-justification, or possibly a seemingly innocent misinterpretation. But the denial of Christ is the same. That means that every 'Christian' person who alters the meaning of grace is actually denying the very Savior they claim to follow. Did you just feel the path get a little narrower? The sad truth is that this is what Christendom has become in our generation. If you are just now joining me, welcome to reality.

Looking at Romans 6:1, the question is posed: "Are we to continue in sin that grace may increase?" This question makes little sense if grace is mere mercy. If, on the other hand, we are diligent to uncover the hidden truth of grace – the question becomes illuminating. Are we to keep separating ourselves from God in sin and expect His life-changing influence to have effect on us? No. The very purpose of His influence on our hearts is to change us, to help us *stop* sinning. You can even apply this truth to your current situation. If God is trying right now to influence you to see that grace is more than mercy and you choose to reject and disbelieve it – can you expect Him to continue to try to convince you? The answer in the Scripture is again no.

The difference in individual personal reactions is the key. Some choose to reject, some choose to trust. Those who trust are like the followers in Acts 18:27 who "believed through grace." God revealed Himself to them, and they believed the truth. He spoke and influenced; they trusted and changed. In Romans 11:5, it says that God reserves for Himself a remnant of followers – chosen by grace. Not by mercy. Not because of a religious makeover. Not because someone prayed and felt sorry. God's choice is based on your choice. Do you respond to His changing influence? Because He reserves for Himself a people who do.

These very people not only hearken to the grace of God, but also continue in that changing influence. The believers in Acts 13:43 were urged to "continue in the grace of God." This is not a one time feel good with God – regardless of how intense the religious moment. Nor is it a life long series of devotional studies. Although these are not wrong in themselves, to continue in the grace of God is to be consistently living under His influence.

This type of heart is rare and uncommon. Few recognize God's hand guiding them to change, much less the Spirit of His grace that is present in every moment. This is the same grace by which the New Testament believers stood (Romans 5:2), and it is the same grace by which *we* can stand. The question is – do you recognize the grace given to you? Do you perceive that God is trying at this moment to transform the way you see the truth? It is so easy to surrender to doubt and skepticism when it seems like the truth is on the opposite side of the world. But please know that God is near you, and He will give you all the grace that you will need (II Corinthians 9:8). And it is my prayer that you will not miss this changing influence of our God (Hebrews 12:15).

Application Summary

Grace is the changing influence of God toward you. It is active and engaging. This influence of God instructs and enables you to say no to all ungodliness. Therefore, the changing grace that brings true salvation is more than mercy. To hold to the concept that grace is only mercy is to believe a lie that will do you spiritual harm. As a matter of fact, to change the true nature of grace is to deny Jesus Christ Himself. But the good news is – God is influencing you, and you don't have to stay the same. You *can* be changed. If you refuse to change, you will have received His grace in vain. This will be empty and meaningless to you. Instead, be humble, or God will oppose you. Grace does not influence you so you can arrogantly do your own thing, but rather it works in you so you will humble yourself and do God's thing. If you continue in His changing influence, He will give you all the grace that you will ever need. Just don't miss the opportunity of being changed by the grace of God.

Challenging Your Perception

1. Are you able to acknowledge the truth that you must be changed by God in order to be saved?

2. Do you find that you alter the definition of grace by turning it into mercy? When Scripture says that to alter grace is to "deny Jesus Christ" – are you honest, or do you waffle?

3. Are you willing to let God's influence change you?

Endnotes

1. James Strong, LL.D., S.T.D., *The New Strong's Exhaustive Concordance of the Bible*, Dictionary of the Greek Testament, copyright 1990 by Thomas Nelson Publishers, page 77, Greek #5485, *charis*.
2. Spiros Zodhiates, TH.D., *The Complete Word Study Dictionary New Testament*, D/B/A AMG Publishers, copyright 1992 by Spiros Zodhiates and AMG International Inc., page 1469, Greek #5485, *charis*.
3. Ibid., page 1088, Greek #3811, *paideuo*.
4. Ibid., page 563, Greek #1653 *eleeo*, page 564, Greek # 1656, *eleos*.
5. Ibid., page 669, Greek #2098, *euaggelion*.
6. Ibid., page 856, Greek #2756, *kenos*.

Sometimes people use the word faith to mean pretend – you know, like saying, "I'm set free by faith," and then pretending you're free when you're not. That isn't faith. That's a sad joke.

Keith Green

Many people claim to be right with God because they can't come to grips with the alternative.

Jeff Baron

We don't renounce from the heart what is shameful without first being truly convinced that it is shameful.

Joe Ford

God conspires with willing souls.

Clement

Chapter 5

AN AUTHENTIC FAITH
(Deeper than Mental Acknowledgement)

"So, then, faith cometh by hearing, and hearing by the word of God."
Romans 10:17(KJV)

What a strange, sleepless night. Morning comes early with the peculiar reality of a communicating artifact still confounding our hero's intellect. And to add to it all – now he is exhibiting the beginnings of a feverish chill. It must have been something he ate. After all, that outdoor café couldn't have been the cleanest. But he knows this is something more, something outside of himself. The hero turns and again perceives that the stone is still glowing. The sounds that were so foreign to his senses before are now steadily simplifying into one clarified thought: the Forbidden Zone.

What? He must be crazy! No one goes into the Forbidden Zone. Those who have entered it over the past several years have never been heard from again. To enter that region of the jungle is to never return. Besides, how could he possibly give any weight to a thought like that in the first place? Is he actually going to trust the guidance of a rock over his own understanding? Yet he

63

feels within himself the ancient language of the Giant Ruby overwhelming his best excuses. He has to go to the Zone. That's where he will discover the answer to this impossible enigma. That's where he will find his . . . purpose. The hero now believes this perilous journey is the direction that destiny is leading him. Forbidden or not, he heads for the Zone.

ೞഃೞഉ൲ೞഃೞഉ൲ೞഃೞഉ൲ೞഃೞഉ൲ೞഃೞഉ൲

Responding to God's direction to walk His ancient path is just as daunting. In this generation, to trust a voice outside of yourself is to be considered odd, if not crazy altogether. Even as a minister, to declare openly your desire to hear and trust the voice of God is considered eccentric. To actually follow through with it – is occupational suicide. This does not change the fact that God is influencing us to find and respond to Him. To continue to pursue such a challenging course necessitates more than just positive reinforcement and pious opinion. It will require an authentic faith.

Abraham was a righteous man who followed God. His encounter with God came almost 430 years before God gave the Law to Moses (Galatians 3:17). In Genesis 18, God promised Abraham a miracle son through his elderly, barren wife Sarah. Although it was hard to believe, he trusted God and received the promised child, Isaac. However, a few years later God asked Abraham to build an altar and sacrifice this miracle child to Him. Abraham agreed in faith knowing God could raise the boy from the dead. But before the knife struck, God spoke in the moment that *now* He knew Abraham's heart. A ram was replaced as the sacrifice, and to this day Abraham is considered the father of our faith.

Surely the concept of a speaking God was foreign to him, and yet he found a relationship that was beyond what anyone around him experienced. The miracle phenomenon of a child born to an old, barren woman was beyond imagination. And for Abraham to offer up his only son, and then receive him back – with God's blessing – must have been amazing.

The Scriptures say that, "Abraham believed God and it was credited to him as righteousness" (Romans 4:3). A few verses later it is stated that he was considered righteous due to his faith. The point is that Abraham had faith and believed what he was told. Because Abraham chose to trust the promises *spoken* to him (Galatians 3:16), God determined that his heart was right. It was Abraham's trust in the voice of God that made him right with the Father.

The intriguing issue at hand is that the only thing needed for Abraham to find God – was God and Abraham. Again, this was hundreds of years before the Scriptures were written and thousands of years before any spiritual tract was printed on how to get saved. There was no church building, no song service, and no visitation ministry. There were no intercessory prayer meetings, pews, or preachers. It was just his ear and God's voice.

This pathway to God came before any other method, and it has *never been invalidated* (Galatians 3:17). Even today – to be right with God comes by faith. To trust the voice of God as Abraham did should be the goal of every living person. What an opportunity – to have a real trust relationship with God that is free from yourself. Was he perfect? No. But God said he was right with Him. Did he do a million religious things to win acceptance? No. Abraham's faith was what pleased God. As a matter of fact, Hebrews 11:6 says that "without faith it is impossible to please God." We need faith to be right with God.

Authentic faith is *pistis*: a persuasion, conviction, and belief in the truth.[1] Therefore to have this faith persuasion is to be convinced by the truth. Remember that truth is far more than just doctrines or 'truths' found in the Bible. Truth is the reality of all things as seen by God. Thus, when you are persuaded, you are being influenced by the reality revealed to you. No longer will you follow your own understanding because you will be changed by God in how you see, how you perceive. If you have faith – a deep, full confidence that relies heavily upon the truth – you posses the unveiled reality of God. It means you are fully persuaded and convicted by the same perception as that of the Father. This becomes your faith.

A person who owns this type of faith will then actively believe. As we have discussed in chapter 3, believe is *pisteuo*, meaning to trust. Just as the Greek word *pisteuo* actually comes from the word *pistis*, so the action of believing comes from faith. Trust is the action of your persuasion. When you are persuaded and convinced deeply, you *will* trust. You don't have to struggle, flounder, or fall short in your attempt to believe. Why? You are fully convinced. It is only when you refuse to agree with God that you will struggle to believe. When this is so, the problem really isn't a trust problem as much as it is a persuasion problem – a perception problem.

An authentic faith persuasion is authentic in that it must be your own, and it must be from God. You cannot cling to the belief of your parents, trust the faith of your pastor, or be swayed by the perception of your friends and still be found right with God. You can neither possess faith vicariously through someone else, nor be a proxy for any other. A full persuasion in God will not come by the influences of well-meaning men, but rather only through the genuine influence of God. It must be *your* conviction. And it must come honestly. Only then will it be real; only then will you be found right.

Now, faith is more than a mere mental acknowledgement that holds deceptively to its own understanding. Convincing your mind that you agree is a completely different thing than your heart being won over by God. Such intellectual assent is shallow and pale compared to the profound intensity of authentic faith. Some even trust in their own lack of doubt. This is complete folly. Never will those who are the Exception be found chasing after some sort of easy believism that lets them put on a mask and parade around as if they were genuine. True followers desire an authentic faith, and it only comes from God.

So, then, faith cometh by hearing, and hearing by
the word of God.

Our main verse, Romans 10:17, states that faith comes from hearing the word of God. Faith, the deep conviction from which you trust – comes from God. More specifically: hearing the *word* of God. The word for 'word' is *rhema*, meaning that which is spoken, particularly as uttered by a living voice.[2] Thus, your faith comes by hearing God speak to you. As our ability to trust comes from faith, so it then follows that our trust comes from hearing the voice of God.

If the gravity of the situation has yet to strike you, let me help. Since according to Ephesians 2:8 you are "saved by grace through faith," then your salvation is completely dependent on God speaking to you – and you trusting His voice. To make my point even further, follow me in this: If you don't hear the voice of God, you cannot trust; if you cannot trust, there will be no grace given to you; if there is no grace given to you, there will be no salvation; if no salvation, there will be no relationship with God; no relationship, no heaven; no heaven means – hell.

Maybe now you will be able to understand my total frustration with supposedly qualified Bible teachers when they do injury to the truth found in Romans 10:17. They have caused the term 'word of God' to traditionally come to mean 'the Bible.' Therefore when this misrepresentation is read by 99.9 percent of all Christendom, people will erroneously think that their *faith* comes from the Bible. Why is that so bad? Because your faith doesn't come from a book – even the best book in the world. It comes from the Living God. *He* said so.

Well, isn't the Bible inspired? Yes. Isn't it from God? Yes it is. Isn't it the 'word of God'? Not according to the Bible. The Bible never calls itself 'word.' The Bible calls itself: the Law, Moses, the Prophets, Scripture, and Holy Writings. These are all words that indicate something that has been *written down*. Even the term 'Scriptures' comes from the word *grapho*, to write.[3] As a matter of fact, except in *very* rare occasions, every place you see the word 'word' in a Bible – Hebrew *and* Greek – it means a spoken word. So understand that when you read 'word' in the Scripture – God made sure it meant a spoken word. Yes, even *logos* means both the act of speaking and the thing spoken, as uttered by a living voice.[4] Realize that God Himself spoke of this distinction when He said to Jeremiah that He would bring disaster on those who "have not listened to My word, and as far as My Law they have rejected it also" (Jeremiah 6:19). And while there is no doubt that God speaks through the Bible, the fact is that without His Spirit revealing the truth to you, you will glean nothing accurately (I Corinthians 2:14). My goal here is in no way to diminish the Scriptures, but to stop the deceitful attempt to weaken the authority of the voice of God.

This concern is nothing new to the world. Even Jesus struggled in the same way to convince religious people that their faith had to be in God, not the Scriptures. He said in John 5:39-40, "You search the Scriptures because you think that in them you have eternal life; it is these that testify about Me; and you are unwilling to come to Me so that you may have life." Searching the Bible for truth is not wrong. Deifying the book above the voice of God is.

So again I say, your faith does not come from a book. Although the Bible is the "God breathed" spoken truth of God that has been written down – *and* is an extremely useful tool (II Timothy 3:16), it will remain only a collection of letters unless the voice of the Spirit of God makes it alive *to you* (I Corinthians 2:14). And know this, we are not meant to find 'life' from our own understanding or interpretation of the Bible (I Peter 1:20); instead we are to live on every spoken "word that proceeds from the mouth of God" (Matthew 4:4).

As if all this falsifying wasn't bad enough, you will find several bibles that translate faith as coming from preaching the message of Christ. Someone just made that up. The translators have no understanding of the verse, so they infect it with the hand of man. Now apparently, according to them, our faith comes from the preaching works of men and *not* from God. May it never be so! It is definitely true that God can speak through men and women, just as Titus 1:3 says that God manifested His spoken word through Paul's preaching about Christ. But Paul would never claim a damnable doctrine that faith came from what *he said*. He was the one who wrote down that faith comes from hearing God speak in the first place!

The truth is that because God can speak to anyone in any part of the world – they can find God and hear His voice in faith just like Abraham did. They can find God even when men grow silent. And a speaking and influencing God can reveal Himself even if the Scriptures are not translated into the language of the person seeking Him. While an immoral country can outlaw the printing and reading of the Bible, they will never be able to silence the voice of the Living God.

Well-meaning – or wicked – many religious leaders are leading the masses down a broad road to destruction as they arrogantly raise their Bible in their hands on Sunday and claim that *it* is their final authority. I'm sorry, but God *is* – and always *will be* – the final authority. It is because men continually do this kind of harm to the Scriptures that I honestly fear that most professing 'Christians' believe in a mute God. Let me just say that if any of this information is new to you, it may be time to perceive the possibility that you've been lied to.

In an attempt to be thorough, look at John 17:17. While Jesus was praying He asked the Father that we would be sanctified in truth and that "Your word is truth." God's *spoken* word is truth. So as God speaks, He is unveiling reality before you. When He speaks, the *spoken* word is "living and active and sharper than any two-edged sword" (Hebrews 4:12), and able to pierce you deeply in the soul. Let this happen. If the voice of God is allowed to apply truth to your heart, you will be persuaded to trust. This shows that even in its very definition that faith – a persuasion, conviction and a belief in the *truth* – is a trust in the voice of God.

Since faith comes by hearing that voice, it is critical we learn to perceive the voice of God. Jesus, who was God in the flesh, said, "My sheep hear My voice" (John 10:27), and that His sheep will not follow the voice of a stranger (John 10:5). To be sure, there are other voices that call out, but none of which influence us to die to selfishness and trust God.

As we have discussed, God is speaking continually through creation and has even offered His grace influence to all mankind in a wide variety of ways. He reveals Himself diversely through dreams (Job 33:15-18, Acts 2:17), visions (Acts 11:15), words of knowledge, words of wisdom (I Corinthians 12:8), discernments (I Corinthians 12:10), and the good old-fashioned gut 'knowing' (Matthew 9:4). He can speak to all your senses – even audibly if He wants to. He's God.

Learning to recognize His voice for the first time is much like talking to an acquaintance on the phone.

> *The phone rings . . .*
> You: Hello?
> God: Hi.
> You: Who is this?
> God: You may not remember me, but this is God – we
>   met the other day?
> You: Oh, yes. How are you?
>
> *The phone rings . . .*
> You: Hello?
> God: Hey, it's God.
> You: God? Oh yes, nice to hear from you again.
>
> *The phone rings . . .*
> You: Hello?
> God: You'll never guess what happened today.
> You: Coming from you, I'd have to agree.

It is a gradual learning to distinguish His voice. As a child learns to listen and trust his father, so a new follower learns to discern the voice of God. As He leads you and influences you, it becomes possible to be aware of the Living God in every moment. And once you begin to hear Him and become familiar with His heart, you will become persuaded to trust.

Proverbs 4:7 (NIV) says that "Though it cost all you have, get understanding." While it is not absolutely necessary to *fully* understand God to trust Him, it is clearly important. Quite often God will speak straight forward indicating His will and desire for you. At other times, His language may seem strange, filled with a variety of symbols and metaphors. Most dreams and visions can seem more like a movie filled with riddles than the voice of God. And, just as the disciples needed help understanding the parables of Jesus, so you too will need the revelation of God. But be encouraged in the fact that God "reveals His thoughts to man" Amos 4:13 (NIV), and "does nothing without revealing His plans to His servants" Amos 3:7 (NIV). When God speaks to you, He will help you understand and trust Him – *if* you will seek wholeheartedly.

Now, I am continually amazed at the ability of God's voice. He is more than able to reveal His will in any moment or circumstance. Circumstances, however, are not the voice of God – though He may speak through them. An event or situation should in no way be misconstrued as indicating the Lord's will without Him saying so. To imagine God is speaking through every incident is to foolishly put your trust in a presumption of your own self-perception. Placing these imagined words in the mouth of God is nothing more than to counterfeit His will in order to religiously fake faith and obedience. This should strongly be discouraged.

I have been urged on more than one occasion to be careful hearing God since people who 'hear God' kill people and say – God told them to. That argument is like saying: A person who drinks and drives will wreck his car, so when I drive I'll wreck my car too. The solution isn't not to drive; the solution is not to drive under the influence of alcohol. The reality is that these insane killers didn't hear God; they just used God as their excuse while they did as they pleased under the influence of self.

When my first daughter was in kindergarten and didn't want to be wrong, she would fib and say that her teacher told her so. In the same way, God has been the excuse for multiple generations to act as they please. But God never leads us to a selfish choice. The 'don't be crazy by hearing God' reasoning is nothing short of an attempt to reject following God in the first place. And the opportunity to reject can be deceptively subtle. All it takes is a . . . "I mean come on, am I really expected to hear and understand God?" And just like Adam who once rejected God's voice himself – you will abandon the ancient path and no longer choose to walk with God. You will find another way; a false way.

So where does a false faith come from? Does it come from what your parents tell you as a child? Thanks Mom and Dad, but wouldn't it have been healthier if you had taught your child how to find God instead? Does false faith come from the teaching of a trusted minister? Thank the Right Reverend for me, but wouldn't it have been far better if he had taught you how to trust the voice of God? Does a false faith originate when you tell yourself all of the available facts and decide upon a conclusion? Well, be polite and thank your 'self' – but to be convinced like that is self-deception and is nothing more than mental acknowledgment run amuck.

Authentic faith should come from the reality that *God* spoke *to you*, revealing to you the truth of your life. It then becomes your choice to hear that word and be so convinced that God completely alters all of your perceptions. I know for a fact that it is better to be considered a wacko nut job for walking God's path and saying God speaks to you than it is to find yourself standing in opposition to the Ruler of the Universe.

You may not think you are opposing God by not 'faithing,' but you are. As a matter of fact, you are sinning. The Greek definition for sin is defined by several different words. To avoid total confusion, let me give you the basics. To sin is to miss the mark. Not just miss it – but to choose to swerve from it. This choosing to swerve results in missing the true end and scope of our lives – which ultimately is a relationship with God.[5] Now, Romans 14:23 says that "everything" . . . I repeat . . . "everything that doesn't come from faith is *sin*." Meaning everything you do, if it is not part of a trust relationship with the voice of God, is your choice to swerve and miss the mark.

It is at this moment that some people ask a revealing question, "You mean I have to hear God to brush my teeth?" Do you see the five telling words? *I have to hear God.* It's a perception issue. The truth is you *get* to hear God speak to you about everything. It is almost as if you can have a day by day, moment by moment relationship with God! In point of fact, that's exactly what it's like.

Make no mistake, though you will never be forced to listen to God, you will be held fully accountable for every word spoken to you (John 12:48). Did you catch that? Whether you follow God or not, you will still be accountable for every single word that He speaks to you. If you want to remain in control of your life, He will let you. You can ignore the original ancient path altogether if you choose. You can even turn around right now and go find someone to tickle your ears and to teach you something that is easier, something that sounds more pleasant. I just thought I was speaking to an Exception – my bad.

Ultimately, there is one way to be righteous with God, and it is revealed from *faith to faith* (Romans 1:17). That means to be right with God we must walk with Him moment to moment, listening and trusting to His every guiding word. This, quite often, is learned by unlearning. By that I mean letting go of all your previous opinions and perceptions that hinder you in having a hearing ear. It becomes possible to trust the voice of God only once you have ceased to trust in your own voice. After you have trained your ear to hear, you can know His will and trust it entirely. To trust His voice from one instance to the next – is to choose to never leave His side.

A person who is not convinced of these things, however, is already walking a path away from God. Hebrews 4:2 says "the word they heard did not profit them, because it was not united with faith. . ." The enlightening truth spoken to them was of no value – wasted on their hardened hearts. Why? A simple refusal to trust what they were told caused the influence of God to have no effect. Now separated from God by choosing to hear a different voice, they have taken a tainted faith – choosing to trust something or someone else entirely.

Now there may be those who, after reading these verses, might twist the Scriptures to say that since faith is found in the voice of God, there is no need for Jesus. To do so would be the gravest of all errors. First of all, God is one God who manifests

Himself to us as a Father, a Son, and a Holy Spirit. So, in reality the voice of Jesus is *also* the voice of God. Secondly, without Jesus' death as a penalty for all sin, there would be no removal of the separation that exists between God and man – thus there would be no opportunity for eternal relationship. And thirdly, without Jesus as our example, we would not be able to take His death as our own and be delivered from the dominion of sin. We would forever be in bondage to the sinful flesh. So, if not for Jesus, mankind would have no hope. If somehow you believe differently than this, I urge you to listen to the voice of God – He will confirm this truth to you if you have ears to hear.

I want to encourage those who do hear "to grow strong in the faith" (Romans 4:20). Trust those things that God is speaking to you and allow them to influence you deeply. Since God speaks to a listening heart, be the heart that listens. There is no list of sins to repent from; there is no set of man-made rules to follow; and though there be countless self-help books ready to deceive you – ignore them all. There is only you and God. To find Him in authentic faith is to know Him. If you will find God honestly, you will need no man to teach you (I John 2:27). There is only one faith and one God (Ephesians 4:5); find them both.

Application Summary

You can be right with God the same way that Abraham was: Hear and trust what God speaks to you. If you have faith, your perception is changed by God, and you will be fully persuaded by the reality He speaks to you. When you have an authentic faith, you will actively trust the voice of God. A trusting faith is more than accepting a mere mental acknowledgment. And although the Bible is the *written* truth of God, your faith only comes by hearing the *spoken* truth of God. Since this faith is needed as a condition to receive the grace of God for salvation, trust the voice of God. If you are the Exception, you will not try to get your faith from the Bible, your parents, or well-meaning preachers – you will get it directly from

God. That is how you will develop a real relationship. Avoid counterfeit faiths, and ignore the people who will call you crazy. Learn to trust God from one moment to the next, and grow deep in the faith as you go.

Challenging Your Perception

1. Are you able to acknowledge the necessity that in order to be right with God you must hear and trust His voice?

2. Do you find that a relationship built only upon the Bible falls short of an engaging relationship built upon hearing and trusting the Living God? In fact, do you see how a belief system – *any* belief system – which is not from God is sin?

3. Do you *have* to hear God, or do you *get* to? Are you willing to shut out every other voice – including your own – in order to please God?

Endnotes

1. Spiros Zodhiates, TH.D., *The Complete Word Study Dictionary New Testament*, D/B/A AMG Publishers, copyright 1992 by Spiros Zodhiates and AMG International Inc., page 1162, Greek #4102, *pistis.*
2. Ibid., page 1262, Greek #4487, *rhema.*
3. Ibid., page 382, Greek #1124, *graphe*, page 383, Greek #1125, *grapho.*
4. Ibid., page 924, Greek #3056, *logos.*
5. Ibid., page 129, Greek #264, *hamartano*, page 130, Greek #266, *hamartia.*

God doesn't need someone who tries –
He needs someone who will.

Joe Ford

Compromise is that inner whisper of the self-life that would turn us from the path of total, unswerving obedience to the will of God.

Arthur Wallis

It is only a question of yes or no, of obedience or disobedience.

Dietrich Bonhoeffer

Allow yourself one excess: to be excessively obedient.

Fenelon

Chapter 6

A TRUE OBEDIENCE
(What Are You Really Obeying?)

"Whoever claims to live in Him must walk as Jesus did."
I John 2:6

"We must go on foot from here," explains the local guide, hired by the hero to make sense of the treacherous Forbidden Zone landscape. The payment for such a guide was next to extortion and the reputation clearly questionable, but the hero felt an escort was needed considering his fading health. Amid the unexplained fever and chills, the Giant Ruby's call remained persistent. There is definitely a point to all of this, but what? They leave an almost non-existent footpath and forge into a thick hedge that appears more like a towering, fifty-foot wall than a tropical forest. After hacking a small opening, they squeeze through to find the jungle suddenly stop at the edge of a great chasm. The hero and his guide view a seemingly bottomless gorge enveloped by a dense fog that billows from out of nowhere. There in front of them stretches a narrow foot bridge connecting both sides of the expanse. It is old and weathered, consisting of broken wood slats and tattered jungle vines that have been braided into rope. Is the hero actually going to go through with this and do what the stone is asking? He knows that he is. And that's when he hears the click.

Standing behind him with a pistol drawn is the disloyal guide with the treacherous intent of stealing the Giant Ruby. The knapsack switches hands as the craving eyes of the self-seeking guide fill with greed. Ecstatic in his acquisition, the guide shrieks with glee and then, with his free hand, reaches into the sack to seize the Giant Ruby. The sound of elation quickly turns into a horrifying scream as the Ruby heats up to an excruciating temperature. With his hand scorched and searing from the angry stone, the guide releases the artifact and retreats in agony. The hero wastes no time. Snatching the pack, he darts fearlessly onto the bridge and runs headlong across the expanse – entering the Forbidden Zone.

He has done it. Although he could turn back, everything inside of him is urging him on. And with each step further into the Zone, the steady and almost melodic resonance confirms that the hero is now being guided by the Giant Ruby.

CRBARCRBARCRBARCRBARCRBARCRBA

Our hero has taken a considerable step. He has chosen to trust a voice outside of himself – to the point of action. This is the concept of true obedience. He didn't come to the Zone because he was following a list that every good adventurer follows; he didn't come to the Zone because someone told him that the Giant Ruby wanted him to be there; and he didn't come to the Zone because he wanted to make himself feel better. He came to the Zone because he trusted what the stone was speaking to him. He obeyed.

The dilemma is that there are numerous misconceptions about obedience as well as the terms – works and deeds. As is true with many of the other crucial issues of real Christianity, religion has managed to revise the truth of obedience to mean something that man can do on his own *without* God. These deeds are then labeled – FOR GOD – and therefore considered good.

But nothing is good unless it comes down from the Father (James 1:17), regardless of what it is branded. In spite of the seemingly good or spiritual appearance, to perform a deed without it coming from above will result in uselessness. And these worthless deeds are the works of man, not the grace influenced works of God. The fact is that to do the works of God you must believe (John 6:28-29), and therefore – you need God. Paul said, "Nothing good dwells in me" (Romans 7:18), and Jesus Himself said that without Him we could do nothing (John 15:5).

Let's apply this concept to Romans 1:5 where Paul states that his ministry was to call people "to the obedience that comes from faith." What does this verse say of obedience? Simply, that true obedience comes from an authentic faith. And since faith comes from hearing God – obedience is to trust what God speaks to you. Thus any work, deed, or action done in faith is an act of obedience because you are obeying the voice of God. Any other action done for *any other reason* is the work of the flesh, the arm of man. Because everything not from faith is sin (Romans 14:23) – every ministry, church service, cause, and 'good deed' – every action – done outside of *really* hearing and trusting the voice of God is sin. Rather than drawing you closer to God, *your will* is causing you to stray and thus separating you further from *His will*.

These self-willed actions are the antithesis to the influence of God's will and consequently impede salvation. This is why Ephesians 2:8-10 says that a person is saved by grace through faith and not of "yourselves" and that it is "not as a result of works." These "works" are attempts by your 'self' to please God by *doing*. Under this guise of pleasing God, many religious people will even go so far as to do what they want to do and then *say* it was in obedience to God. The notion is acceptable to your flesh – after all, wouldn't God want me to do these good deeds? Well, the reality is that God is real; why not ask Him what His will is rather than sin by lying and assuming that you know? You cannot trust something that you tell yourself and be considered right with God. You must trust what He tells you and obey that instead.

The term W.W.J.D. – meaning "What Would Jesus Do?" – has become a popular phrase in this generation. The idea comes from the book *In His Steps* by Charles Sheldon, written in 1896. The story is about a town of people who apply the concept of asking the question – what would Jesus do in this situation? – and then follow that idea instead of what they would normally do. As a result, the story goes, an amazing revival happens. What a sad piece of fiction. Why should anyone decide – in their own understanding – to follow what they think Jesus *would* do when they can ask Him what *to do*? Jesus is not dead. He is alive and breathing and speaking – revealing His will to anyone willing to listen. Those who refuse to hear but still desire to be pseudo-spiritual don this cloak of religious action. And the entire farce has been swallowed by gullible people thinking that God is pleased with their well intentioned self-works. You can even buy the T-shirt.

> *"Whoever claims to live in Him must walk as*
> *Jesus did."*

This brings us to the main verse of this chapter, I John 2:6, "Whoever claims to live in Him must walk as Jesus did." This is a spiritual litmus test. Do you walk as He walked or are you doing your own thing – dressing it up as obedience? To claim you are saved and following God is one thing, to actually walk as Jesus did is another. Wait a minute, you might be saying, how is I John 2:6 any different than W.W.J.D.? Aren't they the same thing? No. Not even in the slightest. Let's explore the reality of how Jesus actually walked on this earth to help enlighten the understanding of our obedience. This will be fun.

Jesus said He does nothing of Himself (John 5:19). Nothing. He didn't speak to His parents from Himself, He didn't confront the Pharisees from Himself, and He didn't heal a single person – from Himself. As a matter of fact, John 8:28 states that Jesus never even acted on His own initiative – but instead followed the Father. Not once did He follow His own understanding. Not once did Jesus decide what was best. And not once did He ask W.W.I.D. – What would I do? He followed something outside of Himself. He followed God. Well, what does that mean? That means He didn't allow Himself to 'pull God.' When the Scriptures say that Jesus gave up deity to become a humble man – it means just that (Philippians 2:6-8). Although fully God, He lived as a human example for us by trusting the Father. *This* is how He walked.

But Jesus didn't stop there. He obeyed the voice of the Father in "*what* to say and *how* to say it" (John 12:49 NIV). Jesus spoke just as the Father had told Him to speak. He didn't add to it nor take away from it. Even the way Jesus spoke – His wording and emotions – were in obedience to the Father. This choosing to agree with the heart of God was not some magical, super-spiritual ability given only to the 'God Club.' Simply put, Jesus walked as man on this earth, yet did not cling to His own opinions or perceptions. Rather, He obeyed the voice of the Father – just as Abraham did.

And when it came to outright obedience, Jesus did exactly what the Father told Him to do (John 14:31). This was not some fearful, robotic response by Jesus to follow a strict rule given by God. Neither was it a self-righteous reaction in an attempt to please God. It was a heart response of trust. Jesus had no will of His own; *He* was not His own. Jesus belonged to the Father. So when the voice of God was heard, it was trusted and obeyed completely.

Do you want to walk as Jesus walked? To truly live in Christ you *must* walk the ancient path just as He did. But you cannot do it by trying to follow a cleverly conceived acronym. You cannot do it by pious, religious actions labeled as spiritual. No, to walk as He did is to completely empty yourself – die to your *self*. Die to every thought, perception, and desire inside of you. By acknowledging the voice of God and choosing to trust it, He can change you – help you empty yourself and repent. You will find that His changing influence on your heart is effective and trustworthy. Then you will be able to do nothing of yourself. Then you will be able to do nothing on your own initiative. And only then will you be able to speak what God tells you to speak, and say it the way He wants you to say it.

> *Not everyone who says to Me, 'Lord, Lord,' will*
> *enter the kingdom of heaven, but he who does the*
> *will of my Father . . .*
> *Matthew 7:21*

Here is another requirement of God that is largely ignored. Treacherous teachings would explain it away by saying that God understands your struggle and that no one is perfect. So, it is because of that kind of attitude Jesus said in verse 22 that *many* would only *say* "Lord, Lord" – but then live religiously without ever truly knowing Him. Again in Luke 6:46 Jesus asks, "Why do you call me 'Lord, Lord,' and do not do what I say?" He goes on to explain how that person who *does not act on His spoken words* is like a man who builds on sand. That foolish person's world will collapse – with no hope.

You see, it is easy to claim to know God but by your actions actually be denying Him (Titus 1:16). This happens anytime you set aside what God is speaking to you in order to follow your own way – your traditional habits (Mark 7:13). So if you say that you have faith in God, but are not hearing and trusting to the point of obedience – your supposed faith is dead (James 2:14-26). It is no faith at all. Do you think that Abraham's faith, which was credited to him as righteousness, would have had any value if he had not followed through with action? No, he trusted and acted on what he heard. This work of obedience was a follow through of his faith – and therefore proved his trust was real (James 2:21-26). It was only then that God saw and said, "Now I know that you fear God" (Genesis 22:12).

It is a tragic fact that if I stood up in many churches today and declared that I believed everyone should have to *prove* their contrition and *demonstrate* the fact that they have been changed by God – I would be shunned. This is heartbreaking since it is a foundational truth to true Christianity. Paul said in Acts 26:20

(NIV), "I preached that they should repent and turn to God and *prove their repentance by their deeds*." The early church required anyone claiming to follow Christ to prove it. Wow. Guess what? So should we. Great, how do we do that? Easy – have you learned to hear God? Are you trusting what He is saying to you? Are you trusting to the point of full obedience? Are you laying down everything in your pursuit of God? Do you love God with ALL your heart? It gets pretty easy to tell by this point who is and who isn't fully surrendered.

Obedience is not obedience if you don't obey God. All you are doing is the work of man. This means you must cease to labor on your own. Jesus taught us to pray and ask God to "deliver us from evil" (Matthew 6:13). Although the word evil conjures up impressions of demons and hell, it has the same meaning as the root word evil in chapter 2 of this book. It means to labor with all the strength of man.[1] Jesus wasn't teaching the disciples to pray for deliverance from Satan in as much as He was instructing them how to ask for deliverance *from themselves*.

The poison of the addiction to self is why anyone who follows Christ *must* deny himself (Matthew 16:24-27). This is why we are encouraged to take captive every thought we have and make it obedient to Christ (II Corinthians 10:5). The need to obey God instead of self is even why we are told to prove ourselves doers of the spoken word of God (James 1:22-25). Why? Because it is not about us. Only God matters to the Exception. And the Exception is willing to hear *and* obey.

There is, of course, always the temptation to obey God selectively; this is common among the religiously deceived. If I sincerely obey *some* of what God has spoken to me, isn't that good enough? No. Well okay, what if I obey some but then do numerous other things, like feed the poor and do mission work – won't that make up for my short coming? No. All you have done is selectively obeyed God. This is half-hearted and wicked. You must deny yourself, hear and trust His voice, and then do what He tells you – wholeheartedly.

There are some who, while claiming true obedience to the voice of God, obey out of obligation. What I mean is that they obey only because it is expected or required. They have heard the voice of God and even perform the outward act of obedience. The problem is that they do so because they feel that they are required to. They obey out of sacrifice, not out of trust. This is the idea inferred when I Samuel 15:22 says, "To obey is better than sacrifice." Deeds performed with the selfish motive to please God – though well-meaning – are actually forms of dressed-up manipulation. These actions are used to bribe God, fearfully hoping to satisfy His standards. Although they have the form of spirituality, they lack anything actually spiritual. In truth, they are flesh. And since God sees the heart, He is not fooled by the shiny outward appearance.

If the motivation of your sacrificial act is to gain approval, you have severely missed the mark of true relationship with Him. Why? Obedience without faith cannot please God (Hebrews 11:6). The very best, heart-felt, and sincere action offered to God is a wicked, depraved, and immoral offering without trust. Why? "Without faith it is *impossible* to please God" (Hebrews 11:6 NIV). No faith means you didn't hear God; no hearing means it didn't come from God; if it didn't come from God, it came from self; and if it came from self, its origin is from hell – and God dislikes hell – a lot. God cannot be bought, conned, or convinced that a self-centered action is a good one – because it didn't come from Him in the first place.

Once you have the right heart, however, and are genuinely obeying God's voice – your relationship with Him can grow immensely. Jesus declares that those who obey Him are the ones who love Him (John 14:21), to the point that He says *you* are His friend *if* you will obey Him (John 15:14). What better way to end the struggle with sin, self, and the world than to walk the path of friendship with the God who created you? And what if you could go even further and become family? In Luke 8:21, when Jesus was told that His family desired to see Him, He said, "My mother and My brothers are these who hear the word of God and do it." I don't know about you, but I want *that* kind of life with God. Anything else seems so shallow.

The sobering reality is that according to John 3:36, "He who believes in the Son has eternal life; but he who does not *obey the Son* will not see life, but the wrath of God abides on him." Obedience to the voice of God is not an optional activity you do after you've secured the goodies of heaven. According to Scripture, obedience is a requirement to find the life of Christ in the first place. Try as you might to avoid the unpleasant truth, but if you don't respond to the grace of God and obey His voice, the wrath of God abides on your life and on everything you do.

The last point I'd like to make is about the pendulum swing involving obedience. On the other side of the 'works' spectrum is probably the most common of all religion: the action of no action. Can you hear the screams of "Do not handle, do not taste, do not touch" (Colossians 2:21) echo down the church halls? The thought is that by physically and emotionally removing ourselves from worldly places, sights, and sounds we will have pleased God somehow. Now please don't get me wrong, I am in no way advocating worldliness or any form of debauchery. Rather, the Scriptures say that with all their wise appearance, these self-made religious teachings of men have "no value against fleshly indulgence" (Colossians 2:23). This is not obedience. Rules don't deliver you and principles can't save you – serving them will only encumber and enslave you.

When Jesus walked this earth, it was never His goal to avoid the world; it was His goal to be separated from it by having a trust relationship with the Father. He was in the world but clearly not of it. Your goal should not involve being removed from this world – or to be removed from temptation – but rather to have the world and temptation removed *from you*. And if you will trust God to the point of full obedience, it can happen. I pray that Jeremiah 31:33 will become true of God's work in you when He said – "I will put my law *within them* and on their heart I will write it; and I will be their God, and they shall be my people."

Application Summary

True obedience comes from God. You can't invent some good works and then label them – For God. They will not be accepted because true obedience can only spring from faith. Therefore, the only good works are the ones that are initiated by God. Your self-determined actions will not save you, and only obedience from faith will please God. To follow your own understanding by acting out what you think Jesus would have done is wicked. He is real and alive – just ask Him. Walk as Jesus did. Turn totally to God and let Him tell you how to live – even what to say and how to say it. Many will say "Lord, Lord," but won't do what He says. Don't be like that. Instead, prove your repentance by your deeds. Cease to labor with your own strength by denying yourself and obeying what God speaks to you. If you love God you will obey Him and become His friend. Even better, do what He says and become family. This would be so much better for you than to be ensnared by self-made rules and religion that have no real value. Do you really want to be free from this world? Learn to trust the voice of God to the point of complete obedience – and you will be.

Challenging Your Perception

1. Are you able to see that obedience is trusting what God speaks to you – to the point of action? Do you understand how self-motivated sacrifice for God cannot please Him?

2. Do you find that you say "Lord, Lord" – but don't obey what He speaks to you? Do you think your faith has any value when you don't follow through to obedience?

3. Are you willing to walk as Jesus walked – doing nothing of yourself? Will you choose to obey the voice of the Father in

"*what* to say and *how* to say it," or only selectively obey what pleases you?

Endnotes

1. Spiros Zodhiates, TH.D., *The Complete Word Study Dictionary New Testament*, D/B/A AMG Publishers, copyright 1992 by Spiros Zodhiates and AMG International Inc., page 1199, Greek #4192, *ponos*.

The strength to die, inherent in Jesus' sacrifice, led men heroically to accept the way of martyrdom . . .

Eberhard Arnold

When you love God, it will not matter to you what you must suffer on His behalf.

Fenelon

The cross means rejection and shame as well as suffering.

Dietrich Bonhoeffer

Self-love fights with all of its strength to live . . . let all that is not born of God within you die.

Fenelon

Chapter

7

THE CALCULATED COST

(My Gospel . . . Even To)

"For which one of you, when he wants to build a tower, does not first sit down
and calculate the cost to see if he has enough to complete it?"
Luke 14:28

After a three-day walk into the darkened Forbidden Zone with no food, our hero seems strangely energized. With his fever subsiding and the Giant Ruby almost singing to him, the atmosphere has become quite pleasant. The jungle almost magically opens to a narrow foot path among the greenest of knee-high grass. As the hero steadily saunters along, the melodic tune of song birds replaces the cruel noises of the wild. And then out of nowhere, he sees an indigenous village a little ways ahead with some local children laughing as they play. This clearly isn't what he anticipated. He didn't know what he'd find, but he never imagined this.

The children see him and instead of running from him in fear, they giggle and wave him in, as if he were expected. Walking through the village, he sees it is a happy little settlement – not the type of place worthy of the title 'Forbidden Zone.' Moving past the straw huts, he is led to the outskirts of the small community. There, in a large semi-circle, he approaches a hundred smiling faces and a lavish feast prepared in his honor. The feeling he has is indescribable. An elderly man, who appears to be the chieftain, stands up and points to a rock wall behind him. The hero steps forward to see hundreds of giant precious stones of different colors and sizes set in perfect fitting, pre-cut indentations on the wall face. And it appears there are places for hundreds more. This is where the Giant Ruby belonged the entire time. Our hero has been called upon to bring it home. He instinctively removes the mysterious stone from his knapsack and hands it to the old man.

The crowd's shout of jubilation is quickly subdued by the unexpected presence of the hero's greedy guide who has crept in undetected and is now pointing his gun directly at the chieftain. With his burnt hand wrapped in a torn piece of shirt, the exhausted guide anxiously motions to be given the prize. Silence. Not one sound from even the smallest of the villagers. The tension is so thick you could cut it with a . . . machete☺.

What heroic action needs to be done? The hero's standard response would involve quick acrobatics to disarm the villain, rapid Special Forces expertise to remove every bullet from the weapon – with one hand – and then defeat the desperado by using at least twelve different forms of ancient martial arts. But that's not the move to make. His old way of thinking was gone. He knew *he must take the bullet.* But he would die! Probably, and yet it was his fault that the greedy guide had followed him and found the secret way into this haven. Our hero reasons that this is his purpose – though it cost him his life. So he quickly steps in front of the elder, and promptly receives three bullets to the chest.

CRISORCRISORCRISORCRISORCRISORCRISO

Cost is an inevitable certainty in our world. Be it the fifty-cent charge for a Popsicle® from the ice cream truck as a child, to the personal price required to obtain a promotion at work as an adult. Cost is a reality. And this has never been truer than in relation to spiritual matters. While there is no doubt that many will trivialize the cost of following the ancient path, it is to be expected. Yet, no matter how many times the uninformed reject the facts – the truth remains the truth. Our hero came to the conclusion that he must pay the ultimate cost of his life, and so must the Exception.

For which one of you, when he wants to build a
tower, does not first sit down and calculate the
cost to see if he has enough to complete it?

Our main verse for this chapter comes from Luke 14:28, in which Jesus Himself was teaching the concept of cost. It begins with the building of a tower. This would be no small undertaking as it requires a great deal of pre-planning, materials, and ground preparation – not to mention the skilled laborers to do the actual construction. But long before any of those things can even be contemplated, the builder must first calculate the cost of such an endeavor.

The word calculate comes from the small stone pebbles that the ancient Greeks used to count with. The meaning deepens when the root word reveals that it was also the means by which they acquitted a person with a white stone and condemned a person with a black stone. Ultimately, the stone came to signify a vote – a voice.[1] In the process of deciding whether you will or will not build a 'spiritual tower,' you too will choose and cast a vote. The question is – will your calculations determine that it is too costly to follow God wholeheartedly, or will you conclude to gladly expend everything you physically, mentally, and emotionally possess for the kingdom of heaven? Jesus calls upon us to make that hard decision. It begs the question, whose voice will you allow to cast the deciding vote – yours or God's?

In the next verse (29), Jesus makes the point that if you start to build the tower but are unable to finish, you will be ridiculed by all who see it. This is a distressing reality in the church world today. Ever wonder why so many people mock the church in this generation? It is because religious people started to follow God's path only to pull up lame half-way down the road. This was not how it used to be. The early church was feared and respected – so it does no good to spin this by saying the church has always been mocked. It has not. The world can easily observe the sinfulness and lifestyle inconsistencies of people who while professing Christianity live anything but Christian. According to Christ, this ridicule is deserved.

Dietrich Bonhoeffer was a minister who died in a concentration camp under the hand of Hitler's SS. He wrote a highly acclaimed book entitled *The Cost of Discipleship*. In it he talks of the fact that God's grace is not cheap by any standard, but rather is "costly grace."[2] If grace were mere mercy – free with no conditions or accountability – I could understand the glib lifestyle of the wickedly religious. But it is not. To hear and trust in the changing influence of God's grace is to engage Him and lose everything else. Though you will never earn it – nor deserve it – God's influence will cost you everything. Since this cost is calculated on many levels, let's discuss some.

Matthew 13:44 tells of how the kingdom of heaven is like a field. A man finds a buried treasure in it and realizes the immense value of his find. He goes home and sells everything he owns using the money to buy the field and so own the treasure. By his calculations, he came out financially far ahead. Now, it was not Jesus' intent for you to perceive from this verse that you could buy the kingdom somehow or that you could in some way earn it. No, His point was that the governing of God over your life is so much more valuable than everything you could possibly hold dear – and to surrender all for it is a no-brainer.

To be part of the kingdom of heaven is so much more than just going to a great place. It is to join God's eternal kingdom, where He is King, Ruler, and Lord over all. Therefore, there is only one legitimate response to the Lordship of God that is acceptable before Him: total, complete, and absolute surrender. This is true repentance. This is genuine change. And it is so significant and valuable that Paul considered it worth the "loss of all things." Oh that we would have the same heart as Paul who was determined to "count them but rubbish" so that he could gain Christ (Philippians 3:8).

This loss of all things, though difficult, is rewarded. "There is no one who has left house or wife or brothers or parents or children, for the sake of the kingdom of God, who will not receive many times as much" (Luke 18:29-30). The treasure found in God is truly worth the loss of all these, though it may be agonizing in the process.

You see, the path that Christ will lead you to travel down is a very narrow one that few will find (Matthew 7:14). There is only room for you alone on this path. Only you – alone and naked before Him – with no encumbrances. This narrowness is the cause for many to reject God's way and find another, broader road to follow (Matthew 7:13). In the main verse for this book, Jeremiah 6:16, it says that when confronted with the good, ancient path the people plainly replied, "We will not listen" (17). And because the path was too costly for them they never saw the journey's end. Yes, it will cost you to listen honestly, and it will cost you to walk the narrow, contrite path – but will you pay that cost?

This brings us to one of the most fundamental truths of all Christianity, the cost of denying yourself. If you indeed want to follow Jesus, to come after Christ – you must – I repeat – must – deny yourself and take up your cross to do so (Matthew 16:24). This is a deal breaker. All the sincere prayers, heartfelt apologies, and well-intentioned activities done in piety will in no way have any value before the King unless . . . you deny yourself. Costly, I know, but you cannot play god in His kingdom. *You* cannot make the decisions of how *you* want to live, where *you* want to work, or who *you* want to get married to anymore. No longer will *you* decide to quit a job, choose who to be angry at, or who to praise. When I deny myself, I let go of all my rights, of all my wants and desires and every single opinion that I have come to believe in outside of the voice of God. My reputation is no longer something I am willing to serve – I will let it get ruined if God so desires. Even the very right to choose what I deny or when I deny it – I am called upon to give to God. When God speaks and reveals the truth, I deny all of these old perceptions and agree with Him.

The concept of denying self becomes complicated, however, when considering the entanglement of religion. The doctrines of men tend to tighten and strangle a person when the knife to cut away the self draws near. Excuses, defensiveness, and self-justification run rampant when our flesh is threatened by the presence of the influence of God. What did your flesh do when confronted with the true definitions for words such as repent, grace, faith, and word? My flesh hated it. It was not what I was taught by men who I thought were right. But I had to let it all go. I chose to deny what I wanted in order to take what God was giving me. And you know what – God was right the entire time. Go figure.

Our old way of living and perceiving – "the old man" according to Romans 6:6, is to be crucified with Christ. When this happens we will no longer be enslaved to sin and self. We count the cost of putting who we were, who we are, and who we will ever be on the cross – and we put it to death. Every evil deed and labor of man – secular or religious – should feel the pain of the cross. To follow Christ is to completely die to your flesh. And know this, if you don't lose your life – you *will* lose God.

Dying to the flesh involves the death of all the fruits thereof. Now you can try to kill a fruit tree by cutting off every bud that appears – but it just won't work. The fruit is a shadow of the root. You want to kill the tree? Kill the root. The root of every sin, no matter what it is – is self – a choosing to swerve and miss God. If you are not willing to release control over your root, be aware of the choice you have made. You have calculated the cost and come up short. To proceed any further with your spiritual tower is to add to the mockery and justification of a wicked world.

A seed remains a single seed unless it falls to the ground and dies (John 12:24). To die is to lose everything that makes a seed a seed. If it refuses to humble itself and fall all the way down to the lowest place it has ever known, it will never be changed. Half-way down isn't good enough. Almost on the ground is failure. The seed must not only hit bottom, it must continue even further down beneath the dirt – to death. If it holds to its old form, it will never know the potential for life within it. Only when the old, outer hardness is decayed in the ground will the seed scramble to the light and become a living thing. The seed willingly pays the cost.

The cost of knowing God would be far less were it not for the world at large. The world hates the light, hates God, and hates a true believer because of Him (Luke 21:17). There will be times you will be called upon to stick your neck out, as it were, to speak a point of truth as led by God. You will become a target for every self-justifying, offended person within ear shot. Some will attack from afar, others right in your face. You will have to deal with everything from sneak attacks behind your back to full frontal offenses planned in advance to great detail and harboring much malice. If this can scare you off, it should.

Acts 14:22 declares that it is, "Through many tribulations we must enter the kingdom of God." This concept is clarified further when II Timothy 3:12 states bluntly that "all who desire to live godly in Christ Jesus will be persecuted." Two things – *all* and *will be*. There are no exceptions based on gender, race, or education. The amount of money you make does not somehow exclude you from this fact. Funny you don't hear pious, religious people claiming *this* promise when they are feeling spiritually frisky. All . . . will be . . . persecuted. That should thin the crowd a bit.

The good news is only good to those who want to be free from self. The Apostle Paul explained that Jesus rose from the dead "according to *my gospel* for which I suffer hardship *even to* imprisonment as a criminal" (II Timothy 2:8-9). So let's add it up:

My gospel + even to (cost) = suffering

Roman 8:17 states the fact that, "We are heirs of God and fellow heirs with Christ, *IF* indeed we suffer with Him." Not the kind of good news the shallow and cowardly want to hear. But this is the true gospel. Time has not changed it – the wicked doctrines of men have. God's requirements still stand, as do the trials that come with them. If you haven't seen this type of Christianity, maybe it's time to find a new church.

So what of *your* gospel? What type of gospel does your life preach . . . even to? What good news does your life reflect and how far are you willing to go for it? Be careful here, unless God Himself has spoken and revealed the answer to you – you are only guessing. Since there is more than enough assumption in Christendom already, why not just go to God? He knows the truth of your heart – and to what extent you will suffer for the kingdom. Whatever the cost, it will be worth it.

It is truly sad to see how few are willing to stand in the gap and hold people accountable to the truth. Now don't get me wrong; this is not something to decide to do on your own. But, if God calls upon you to do just that – it will fare far better for you if you have already determined that the cost is acceptable. If you haven't, you will fail – because you will either shrink back, or you will handle the situation in the flesh. Half-way through your 'tower,' conflict and your underestimation will cause the world and hell itself to ridicule your stand.

The cost of following God can quite often rear its ugly head right in the middle of your favorite fellowship. There you are – minding your own business trying to follow God with all your heart and Wham! A person with a nasty, false doctrine stares you right in the face. Your flesh voice says avoid it at all costs, the erroneous voices of grace as mercy say let things continue in sin, but then there's Jesus – speaking very clearly that you must speak up. So being a good soldier for Christ, you speak what needs to be said, and now you are the bad guy. Apparently you don't have love in your heart because blah, blah, blah. You shouldn't interfere with other people's faith blah, blah, blah. You are only causing division blah, blah, blah. Been there, done that.

Now, you may find it hard to swallow, but division in the church can actually be a good thing. A good thing?! Yes sir. Remember that whole light divides the darkness concept? In I Corinthians 11:18-19, Paul says something he could get stoned for in most churches today:

> *I hear that divisions exist among you; and in part*
> *I believe it. For there must also be factions among*
> *you, so that those who are approved may become*
> *evident.*

You see, *unity* is not *God*. Anyone can develop a group of people in unity. Only God can influence people to a unity in the truth. The Greek word for factions in this verse is *hairesis*. Look familiar? It should, it means heresy.[3] Because God desires truth in the church, He will allow divisions to become apparent. When that happens, He calls upon these approved ones – who have counted the cost – to stand in the gap. The Exceptions are the types who choose this path of purity regardless of the cost.

Whether inside or outside of the church, there are numerous persons who wait in the wings ready to pick a fight. Counting the cost of following God is the only way to prepare for the possibility of confrontation. If the cost of Christ means I am ridiculed, so be it. If the cost of Christ means I will be abused, let it be so. If the cost of Christ means that I will be reviled by those who think that by killing me they do God a service (John 16:2) – I am ready and my life is in God's hands. One man alone with God is a majority. And he's in good company.

Dietrich Bonhoeffer's most famous quote is – "When Christ calls a man, He bids him come and die."[4] There is no better way to say it. Any form of Christianity that waters down the fact of dying to self and suffering for Christ is not Christian. Matthew 16:25 says, "Whoever wishes to save his life will lose it; but whoever loses his life for My sake will find it." The cost is clear: To be a disciple of Christ you must give up everything (Luke 14:33).

So what's the up side to all of this hardship and difficulty? "Blessed are those who have been persecuted for the sake of righteousness, for theirs is the kingdom of heaven" (Matthew 5:10). This promise reveals that there is a positive side to suffering. Therefore, we would do well to arm ourselves with a mind to suffer. No, I don't mean to develop a martyr's complex that goes out looking for trouble. Actions like that wouldn't be in obedience and therefore would just be following your own desires. Rather, hope for the best – but be prepared for the worst. Just because you are not being persecuted now, doesn't mean you won't be. And just because you may live in a relatively free nation, it doesn't mean that you will always be free from such abuse. Persecution will come to you; it's a promise. But when it does – embrace it.

Ultimately, one day we will all leave this earth. When you do so consider the way in which you exit. If you indeed surrender your entire heart to God by hearing and trusting Him – He will make you right with Him. If so – don't go kicking and screaming into the presence of God. What I mean is that so many people, many claiming a relationship with Christ, fear death as if it were a bad thing. How could the idea of leaving this place of evil and sin and hatred – to see the face of the God we love and worship – ever be a bad thing? No, it will be truly wondrous. Therefore, whether you die in quiet repose or are savagely tortured – die well. To fear death is to fear judgment. That is not faith in the least and proves the reality of a wicked heart that has not counted the cost of death.

In all your calculations of whether or not to follow God, add up just one more thing: When you stand before His holy throne, wouldn't you – at that moment – give anything to be right with God?

Application Summary

Cost is a certainty in life, the question is – what are you willing to lay out for it. Every day your heart makes cost decisions, but to find the kingdom of God you will need to go deeper. Choosing whether or not to follow God requires that you take the time to calculate what it will cost you personally. If, in the process of counting what you are willing to surrender, you decide that it is too costly to continue – fine. But to start following God only to later second guess yourself – regretting the decision you made – will only result in ridicule. And rightly so. Far too many pretend in dishonesty that they are okay with God while refusing to give up their lives to have a relationship with Him. Will this be you? Will it be too costly for you? The road you are required to follow is narrow and difficult. Suffering is guaranteed. But the treasure of God is worth it all. You must learn to deny yourself in the same way Jesus taught the disciples to die to themselves. Kill the fruit of outward sins by killing the root of your inward sin and selfishness. Become like a seed that lets go of its form for something far better. It is true that the world will hate you. You will even discover the world hiding amidst everything from your family to your church. Even your best friends will pass you by because you want to go deeper. Let them. The question is will you be willing to be a true disciple of Christ . . . even to? Even to losing your friends, your family, and your job? Even to the loss of money, reputation, and health? Even to your death? Will you choose God over everything else, holding nothing in reserve? Every true believer has. Every true Exception will as well.

<u>Challenging Your Perception</u>

1. Can you see how religious people *claim* to love God with 'everything,' but in reality, they keep what they want, refusing to surrender what is most precious to them?

2. Do you find that when circumstances make it difficult to follow the voice of God that you back away from doing what is right because of the cost?

3. Are you willing to embrace a mind to suffer . . . even to? Are you willing to pay the personal price of being called crazy, a heretic, and a cult member in order to follow Jesus – or is it just too costly for you to follow God wholeheartedly?

Endnotes

1. Spiros Zodhiates, TH.D., *The Complete Word Study Dictionary New Testament*, D/B/A AMG Publishers, copyright 1992 by Spiros Zodhiates and AMG International Inc., page 1493, Greek #5585 *psephizo*, Greek #5586 *psephos*.
2. Dietrich Bonhoeffer, The Cost of Discipleship, The Macmillan Company, second edition copyright SCM Press Ltd reprint September 1964, page 35-47.
3. Spiros Zodhiates, TH.D., *The Complete Word Study Dictionary New Testament*, D/B/A AMG Publishers, copyright 1992 by Spiros Zodhiates and AMG International Inc., page 98, Greek #139, *hairesis*.
4. Dietrich Bonhoeffer, The Cost of Discipleship, The Macmillan Company, second edition copyright SCM Press Ltd reprint September 1964, page79.

*What is a religion good for that does not overcome the world?
What good is a new birth that fails to bring us into a likeness of
God . . . that leaves us in bondage?*

Charles Finney

*You can't soften the gospel to adapt it to your weakness. Woe to
anyone who tries to widen the narrow way.*

Fenelon

*It's scary to realize that some people will go before the judgment
seat of God convinced that they are going to Heaven – when they
are not.*

Keith Green

*Let nothing short of a radical change of heart satisfy you in your
converts.*

William Carey

Chapter
8

A CERTAIN SALVATION
(Or Hell-bent On Going to Heaven?)

"For by grace you have been saved through faith . . ."
Ephesians 2:8

The final crack of the third gunshot echoes throughout the countryside seemingly forever. Our hero's lifeless body lays slumped at the chieftain's feet with the splattering of blood from his chest turning into a small pool on the ground. Stunned, the greedy guide stands wide-eyed and clearly bewildered by the hero's self-less gesture. In an almost instinctive, defensive action he begins waving his weapon around indiscriminately at the crowd. The aggressive and menacing intentions of the guide cause an instant murmuring amid the gathering and mysteriously awaken the wall of sentient stones mounted across the rock face. As if controlled by one thought, the jewels start to glow their varied colors while generating an angry ear-piercing tone. Knowing that this paranormal event is aimed at him, the greed-filled guide turns and then begins firing upon the supernatural gemstones. The glow from each individual jewel begins to unify and gather strength into one magnificent single beam. Then with no warning, the powerful concentrated beam shoots out from the wall directly at the man and –.

Now, if this narrative were a simple fairy-tale, the beam of light would manifest a hologram of an ancient bearded wise man to convey a moralistic allegory to help the guide see the error of his ways. Or if this account were a social satire, the beam would transport the guide to another dimension where everything in his life is reversed causing the guide to dramatically come to his senses. But it is not; this is an adventure tale where the bad guy always gets his – so the magical light beam hits the man square in the face and fries him to a crisp☺.

Since there is nothing left of the bad guy except a little, greasy spot on the ground, the attention of the crowd turns to the Giant Ruby now glowing in the hands of the village chieftain. The piercing resonance from the mystical stones becomes a harmonious composition in which the villagers join in a unified chorus. As the tune of the melodic symphony swells, a rose shaded hue grows from the Giant Ruby to fully encompass our hero. With nothing more than a slight cough, our hero opens his eyes – he's alive! He stands to his feet disorientated, yet fully healed. Now either by a miracle or by a mistake in the wardrobe department, every bullet hole and bloodstain has disappeared from his clothes as he turns and waves to the people. Still amazed by his deliverance, the hero helps the elder set the Giant Ruby into its rightful place on the rock face as a unanimous shout of joy erupts throughout the village. The great feast of thanksgiving has begun.

ᘉᘻᘎᘍᘉᘻᘎᘍᘉᘻᘎᘍᘉᘻᘎᘍᘉᘻᘎᘍᘉᘻᘎᘍᘉᘻ

Salvation – Part I
THE BIG PICTURE

If you would like to know the meaning of life, let me give you the answer here and now and save you that very long climb up the mountain to ask the proverbial 'great guru.' As our hero dramatically illustrated, the meaning of life is death. It always has been. Life only comes through death. Be it the seed of a plant or the seed of a man, only once the seed has died and is liberated from itself will it change and become a living thing. The old must pass away for the new to manifest (II Corinthians 5:17). This is especially true in relation to all things spiritual. In order to know and experience the true life that is found in Christ, you must die to what and who you are – and be changed. Salvation is all about that very change.

In order to accurately explain the depth of salvation, I feel the need to lay some ground work first. In education circles, what I am about to do is called teaching whole-to-part. Simply put, this means to teach a concept as a complete, overall picture – and then fill that picture up with the individual brush strokes that create the whole. So, I'm going to give you a crash course in 'The Big Picture,' and then I will fill in the salvation part after that.

So here we go. God created all things. He created everything that is and is Lord over everything. One day God created the angels, including one named Lucifer. Now, God made Lucifer beautiful and gave him a position of leadership. Lucifer's name means Morning Star, indicating that in his beauty he shined.[1] You must understand that Lucifer, also known as Satan, was given everything. He was made stunning to look at, was given position, and was allowed to live in the very presence of God (Ezekiel 28:11-19). But that apparently wasn't enough. Satan wanted more, like a spoiled rich kid who doesn't know how good he has it. He became puffed up and lusted to be like God and to ascend to the throne (Isaiah 14:13-14). In the process, he convinced a third of the angels to rebel with him (Revelation 12:4), and attempted to take heaven by force (Revelation 12:7). Lucifer failed obviously, and lost his place in heaven when God cast him to the earth (Revelation 12:8-9).

God then decided to create mankind just a little under the angels (Hebrews 2:7) – not giving *them* everything. He did this in order to share a deep relationship with them – thus shaming

Lucifer (I Corinthians 1:27). God was now going to have a very close, very real relationship with beings that were inferior to the boastful Morning Star. Satan in his jealousy and hatred for all things 'God' decided to deceive God's new love by driving a wedge between them. In the book of Genesis, Lucifer deceived Eve, who in turn convinced Adam to disobey God. Satan had found a way to taint God's children with himself by way of sin. When Adam sinned, we all sinned (Romans 5:12), and thus we were all born into that dark dominion of influence. This dominion of separation holds its rule over every human. You were born with no choice but to obey its control, with no power of your own to alter it. Even at an early age, we all display the undeniable selfishness to go our own way; to swerve from what is right.

God however, had no intention of leaving us on our own – bound by sin and separated from Him. So He spoke. God revealed that He was real and that if the world would listen *and* be changed by His influence – it would be set free. God then spoke Himself into existence by being born to walk this earth as a man named Jesus. Though sinless, this Emmanuel ('God with us') suffered death on a cross to pay the penalty for the sin of mankind. By dying and paying this penalty for us, Jesus bridged the gap between God and man so mankind could once again walk in open honesty with Him as Adam once did. For this reason Jesus declared, "I am the way, and the truth, and the life; no one comes to the Father but through Me" (John 14:6).

When Jesus took on this sin He was actually separated from God – literally separated from Himself – for us. His willing death demonstrated what it meant to let go of *yourself.* He then rose again from death to life, revealing the truth that new life can only come from death. Jesus then ascended into heaven and to this day remains our living example of how to walk in a trust relationship with God.

Throughout history, a small minority of individuals has trusted the voice of God and taken Jesus' death as their own – proving that they are genuine Exceptions. Because they are willing to apply the cross of dying to self to their life, Jesus' sacrifice for sin is applied to their hearts. Set free from the bondage of sin, they no longer live under the control of its dark dominion (Colossians 1:13). Gone is the tendency to stray. Now they tend to hear. Now they tend to repent. Now they tend to surrender all. These few who find the narrow road (Matthew 7:13-14) have chosen God over everything else – over every temptation and ploy of the Devil. It really is amazing that man – who is less than the angels, who is born in heart separated and rebellious before God, who must struggle through the harshest of trials of this world – can with the grace influence of God do the one thing Satan wouldn't – choose God.

It is this very fact that infuriates Satan. Imagine how embarrassing it is for him that these 'less thans' will be given a place of honor over himself and the angels on that day (I Corinthians 6:3). Through His delivered people, God will display His manifold wisdom to the rulers and authorities in the heavenly realms (Ephesians 3:10-11) – putting Lucifer to shame for the wickedness of his heart. God is making a people for Himself far different than Lucifer, who have chosen God above all else – *in spite* of all else – and He does it through relationship. This is why you are here on planet earth; it is why you were created by God to exist. It is for His glory and for your benefit. And it is important to know that His purpose, whether you like it or not, is unchangeable (Hebrews 6:17). This is 'The Big Picture.'

So let's fill in the details of this picture. To do so, we will look at the main focal point of our new painting by reviewing the basics of what we have learned up to this point. This is the very crux of the ancient path – the root of salvation. If you learn nothing else in this book – allow God to train you deep in heart pertaining to these things.

As we have studied, all of us were born into sin and thereby separated from God. This sin is a choosing to swerve and miss the mark of obedience to God. We are under that dominion and rule of selfishness with no ability of our own to be delivered out from under it. Seeing our predicament, God in His mercy gives us a way to have Jesus' sacrifice applied to our lives so we can be set free from the chains of sin, self, and separation:

For by grace you have been saved through faith;
and that not of yourselves, it is the gift of God
Ephesians 2:8

The Scripture shows that it is by grace we are saved. Grace is God's changing influence. His influence for repentance and change has gone out to all mankind to teach us to say no to the ungodliness of our lives (Titus 2:11-12). This changing influence of grace saves you only *if* you have faith – because it works through faith.

Faith is a deep trust that is persuaded by God's changing influence. This trust displays an agreement with God in all things. It is a complete dependence on God, manifesting confidence and conviction that He is Lord, that He is all in all. This faith does not come from you. You can not conjure it up or take any credit for having it. It does not originate from any other man either. No preacher can give it to you; no Bible study can develop it in you. Faith comes one way and one way only – from the voice of God (Romans 10:17). This changing and saving influence is God's spoken gift to you.

Your faith, your deep trust – comes by a relationship with Jesus whereby you listen with a 'hearing ear.' Know that God does not speak to you to hear Himself talk; He speaks to you to help you – to save you. (Now I pray that you have perceived and connected the dots on this.) You are saved by God's changing influence (grace) through trusting and being persuaded (faith) in the voice of God. And *if* you are truly hearing and trusting the voice of God, you obey Him (James 2:17). In this you prove your repentance by your deeds (Acts 26:20). You apply what He is speaking to you, deep in the heart to the point of complete surrender. You hear the direction of God and actively trust in complete agreement. No word is too difficult for you. No topic off limits. Not one single syllable uttered in a whispered tone is ignored. His voice is life to you; it is your salvation. You are changed to the point that you live on every word that proceeds from the mouth of God (Matthew 4:4). This repentance and changing influence by God causes you ultimately to love Him with *ALL* your heart. Everything you know and everything you are aware of become His. You are His, and no one else's. True salvation only comes through this kind of trust relationship with God, and it is only then that Jesus' sacrifice removes the penalty of your sin. Review over.

Salvation – Part II
GETTING DELIVERANCE

This wondrous idea of salvation, like so many terms, has been twisted and distorted by religion over the years. Yet unlike other words, it is not the definition of salvation that is the problem – it is the application of it. The word salvation means safety, deliverance, preservation from danger or destruction.[2] And as you would expect, the word saved is the past tense of to save, deliver, make whole, preserve safe from danger.[3] This is pretty much the standard definition in most churches today. But the question is: from what are you saved; from what are you delivered?

A large number of professing believers will tell you they are saved from hell. But among the varied and quite convincing arguments, you will find that the root motive is selfishness to avoid punishment. Now I'm no fool, I don't want to be punished either. But the fear of punishment is not faith. As a matter of fact it is the opposite of faith. Although most preachers would give their right arm to have throngs of people fear hell and thus respond to their altar call, it is not salvation that they would be seeking. They seek self. They seek a preference. They seek a chosen eternal lodging that is pleasant to them, free of difficulty. How is this any different than the selfish way they are living on earth today? No, being saved is more than this.

Then there are those multitudes that claim Christianity and confess that it is heaven they truly seek. Again, this is nothing more than root selfishness. Can you see the self-protection that says, "Just give me eternity where I will be okay, where I will be happy and comfortable?" These misguided individuals are so hell-bent on going to heaven – they miss it altogether. Heaven is not the goal. Never has been. Heaven is only heaven because God is there. If going to heaven is your focus, your perception is tainted and your heart impure. Deliverance is more than the aspiration of going to heaven. Your goal should be God.

Now, moving beyond the selfish desire to free your soul from suffering, let's look at the struggle of being saved from sin. The dilemma many find themselves in is that they know they need to be delivered from sin – but don't want to stop sinning. This flies in the face of "Be holy for I am Holy" (I Peter 1:16 NIV) and "No one who is born of God practices sin" (I John 3:9). And yet the wicked and perverse generations of the past have handed down a dark doctrine to this religious age. Just change the concept of sin a touch. Say yes to being saved, but don't actually remove sin from the life. Make salvation a deliverance only from the accountability, judgment, and punishment parts of sin. This allows the merely religious to claim a guiltless 'salvation' while justifying a lifestyle of sinfulness. But to say that you can be delivered and yet *not* be held accountable for continued wickedness – shows you are not delivered at all. (Throw away those rose-colored glasses; they make you look foolish.)

The truth is that through the voice of God revealing sin to you, you have the responsibility to actually repent of your sin. (Remember: Repentance is more than just feeling sorry, it is to change – to turn *from* the sin *to* God.) You must in reality see your wicked choice to swerve for what it is, and by the grace influence of God choose to let go of that very choice. There is no dodging repentance from sin; there is no evading change. Jeremiah 17:14 says, "Save me and I will be saved." That means this is a real deliverance from sin – not a pretend, hollow, or half-done change to feel okay. You might be saying that it is impossible, but Jesus said it is not (Luke 18:27). True, you will not be able to do it on your own, which is why God speaks, influences, and reveals the truth to you. You must know that you *can be* "saved through the grace of the Lord Jesus" (Acts 15:11).

To be delivered from your sin means exactly what it sounds like – to be delivered. This means that you are no longer under the dominion and control of the self-will. This means you are no longer under the control of the chain that pulls you from the path of God. This means you are no longer under the control – of you. Ceasing to follow your own path and your own choice will no longer be a struggle. God *in every sense of the word* delivers you from the will to go your own way. You don't have to continue to sin anymore. And you don't. Where in the past you had the tendency to sin and go your own way – now you tend to turn to God. Holding nothing back, you willingly surrender every area of your life that you are aware of. You are saved from the dominion of sin and now walk in the dominion of God. The cross will no longer be a pin you wear on your shirt, it will be a lifestyle that lives in your heart. No more separation. No more being swayed by self. No more being controlled by sin. Now that's good stuff.

You may not like it, but I'm going to bring up one of the most deceptive practices of all religion. You might want to sit down for this one. It is the unscriptural, damnable doctrine of the sinner's prayer. (I figure if I haven't lost you yet, you'll hear me out on this.) I believe more Evangelicals from this generation will waltz through the gates of hell because of this false doctrine than from any other. The sinner's prayer is a man-made, watered-down, quick-fix religious work. Yes, I said work. And it *is* unscriptural. What *is* scriptural, however, is the fact that Ephesians 2:9 says that we are saved "not as a result of works," and yet the half-hearted think they are going to heaven as a result of something they *did*. They prayed a prayer. I'm sorry, but if you try to justify your faith relationship with God by putting your trust in something you did – you are deceived and will be damned. A prayer cannot deliver you, so why would you put your faith in such a work? Your trust was never intended to be put in a prayer – it must be in the voice of God.

Am I saying that you shouldn't pray and receive or accept Jesus? Not at all. Any prayer done in sincerity is a good start. But this, in and of itself, is not deliverance. And no preacher should tell anyone that they are saved because they prayed or because they made a decision. A decision is not salvation. Even several hours of 'praying through' to an emotional release means little when it does not produce actual deliverance from daily sin. Freedom from a self-centered lifestyle must take place in order to produce the fruit of repentance. Once deliverance is evident, God will know your heart and *He* will accept *you*. The fact is – God will let His children know that He is their Father; He's good like that.

What about that radical individual who everyone at church knows is fired up for Jesus? I'll be honest with you – the proof is in the pudding. If the radical is truly a follower of God, it isn't because he prayed the prayer. It is because he found God, was truly delivered by Jesus, and God chose him when he trusted in His voice. And if genuine, the radical would agree with these truths. Now, I can't tell you how many 'Jesus freaks' I've met only to discover that they are far more 'freak' than they are 'Jesus.' Even in the pulpits across America, this generation has lost count of how many 'holy' and 'delivered' ministers have fallen because of adultery, embezzling, and other secret sins. If you find yourself wanting to justify their sin for them – don't. Their judgment has been spoken of long ago.

Now, I realize that religious people have a very good reason for ignoring this truth. They reject it because deep down inside they want it to be okay to continue in daily sin. But distorting doctrine to practice sin is not Christianity. It is a fabricated religion made to look like Christianity. And just because you have believed a lie about salvation your whole life doesn't mean it's acceptable to keep doing so. No matter what attempt is made to alter the truth, you will have zero confidence in your salvation until *God speaks to you*. And all the altar calls in the world will not change that fact.

"Well, I put my faith in Jesus when I prayed the prayer." Are you sure? Or is this just what you were told to say by a presumptive minister? Understand that the naïve are never taught to question this honestly before God. No, they are told to never doubt it, insulating them from any possible conviction from the Holy Spirit. They are trained to go back and 'claim' *that day* like it is a sign post to Satan, a stake in the ground confirming the *time* they prayed. But a true follower of God does not trust in an action or a time any more than he would a false prophet. There is only one way to be saved, only one way for the cross to deliver you from the bondage of sin. And that is by trusting the grace influence of God by hearing and obeying what He speaks to you. That is the path to righteousness. That is real relationship with Jesus. Trust Him, not your works. If not, you are refusing to submit to God's righteousness and seeking to establish your own (Romans 10:3). Again let me say, you will only be delivered when you are "saved through the grace of the Lord Jesus" (Acts 15:11).

"But I really meant it when I accepted Jesus!" Well, contrition is fine, remorse is needed, but salvation – actually being delivered – is not secured by you accepting Jesus. (That's got to grind against the establishment!) As I said before, salvation is only secured when Jesus accepts you. Pray and 'receive' Jesus a thousand times a day, but it won't *change* anything. Romans 11:5 very clearly states that God's remnant is *chosen* by the changing influence of grace – not man's acceptance.

This point can be driven home by looking at John 1:12 which says, "But as many as received Him, to them He gave the right to become children of God, even those who believe in His name . . ." You see, you just can't have the "receive" without the "believe." Those who *truly* receive Jesus also *truly* believe – thus proving once again the need to turn and hear the voice of God for a trust relationship with Christ.

The next verse (13) continues by saying that those who receive and believe are "born, not of blood nor of the will of the flesh nor of the will of man, but of God." A person does not become a child of God by deciding one day to be so. Instead, a person becomes a child of God when God delivers him from himself, and chooses to adopt him as His own. Ultimately, "A man can receive nothing unless it has been given him from heaven" (John 3:27). So receive Jesus, but do it *His way* – letting His voice draw you to Himself as you surrender everything He asks of you. Develop a relationship where after you choose God, He chooses you.

The parable Jesus taught in Matthew 22:1-14 teaches this concept to those with hearing ears. So many people were invited to the king's banquet, and yet so many refused to go – giving all sorts of excuses. Then other people, less deserving, were invited in their place, and they actually heard the king's invitation and responded without all the excuses. The banquet hall was filled. Then the king saw one man who *had been invited* – who *had heard* and *responded* – among all the others. Maybe he was sincere; maybe he genuinely received the invitation with gratitude; maybe he really wanted the king to receive him and so he walked the path to the king's door. Regardless, when he arrived he was not in wedding clothes. He was still dressed in his *own* clothes. The point is he had *not changed* before he entered the king's banquet hall. The king confronted him and asked how it was he had managed to enter without changing. The man was speechless. No words, no excuses, no clever doctrinal declarations. No mission statements, no board meeting bravado, no pious justification. Speechless. Then the king ordered that man, who had *refused to change,* to be bound hand and foot and cast into outer darkness. Why? Because "many are called, but few are chosen" (verse 14).

There will be countless people on that day waving their sinner's prayer invitation around like it is a free ticket to heaven. How mistaken they will be. Understand that you *are* one of the 'many' invited. The question is – will you be one of the few who are chosen? To be chosen you must hear what God speaks to you, repent and be changed. This does not come from you; it only comes from the one true God. Thus, entering the kingdom of God is not up to the preacher who mistakenly tells people that they are saved because they prayed a prayer. It is up to the King. In John 13:18, Jesus says, "I know the ones I have chosen" – but *has He chosen you?* And there is only one way to know *for certain*. The King Himself must tell you so. Hear me in this:

There is no other name whereby we must be saved (Acts 4:12), and unless Christ tells you He accepts you – you have no hope. This is exactly why Romans 8:16 states, "The Spirit Himself testifies with our spirit that we are children of God." To have a certain salvation you must hear it from the King's mouth – and then trust it.

Maybe you are a clever Bible scholar who declares Romans 6:23 says, "The wages of sin is death, but the free gift of God is eternal life. . ." It says free gift right there in black and white. I know it does, but it shouldn't. In the Greek, "free gift" is the word *charisma*.[4] Part of the word is *charis* (grace), which amazingly is ignored in most translations. Thus the word is better defined as 'grace gift.' Now let's re-quote the last part of that verse again: "The grace gift of God is eternal life. . ." Ah, means something much different now doesn't it? Interesting too is that the suffix *–ma* indicates the result of grace.[5] So if we take Romans 6:23 one more time and insert everything we have gleaned so far, it reads: "The wages of choosing to swerve and miss God is death, but the result of God's changing influence is eternal life. . ." Hey, I'm not making this stuff up.

"But aren't grace, faith, and salvation free?" Free, but conditional. Grace has appeared to all mankind (Titus 2:11), but only those who trust will benefit from it (Ephesians 2:8). Faith is available to everyone, but a trust that doesn't follow through to obedience is a dead faith (James 2:20). And salvation, though clearly offered to every person ever born, must be a personal application of true deliverance from all self-will, self-choice, and self-centeredness. You can't just be given salvation; your life must be altered to *live* salvation. Deliverance is more than a fleeting, religious absolution of guilt and obligation that produces no power to change. And though it is absolutely true that salvation cannot be earned, make no mistake – it will cost you everything to obtain it. These truths are found all through the Scriptures, if you just have the heart to seek them out.

I want to transition to another word closely associated with salvation: forgiveness. Once again there can be little doubt that religious people, in a malicious attempt to sneak through the narrow gate, have taken this valuable concept and wrenched it sideways. To most, the term forgiveness from sin means to no longer suffer punishment for sin, to no longer be held accountable for past or future transgressions, and thus to no longer be under the hand of guilt because of sin. The problem is that this type of forgiveness omits the actual removal of the sin. This is where pathetic statements like, "I'm just a sinner saved by grace" come from. When you are *actually* delivered by grace through faith – you won't need a clever bumper sticker to justify your wickedness.

This brings up the point at hand. There are a number of Greek words that are used throughout the Bible for forgive. Let me give you an overview of some: *aplouo*, to let loose, unbind;[6] *aphiemi*, to send forth or away, let go from oneself;[7] *aphesis*, remission, the putting away of sin and deliverance from the power of sin.[8] Now all these words involve the fact of being let loose from sin or sending sin away. Understand: Being forgiven – let loose from sin or having your sin removed – is far beyond the idea of just being pardoned and no longer having to be held accountable. Forgiveness means that your sin is *removed*. The heart that chooses to swerve and miss the voice of God is *taken away from you*. Now – in every moment – you can trust God's voice because the dominion of choosing to be separated from God has been broken. This is the truth of forgiveness on the ancient path.

Let's look at one more word to round out the idea of forgiveness. *Charizomai* has been translated as forgiveness a few times in the Bible and is an interesting study for the person with an inquisitive eye. Our respected Greek scholars have defined this word as favor.[9] Yes, forgiveness has within it favor, but do you see what I see? The root word for *charizomai* is grace. And though scholars may agree with the presence of the root word and even agree with the idea of 'favor,' it is notable that the *rest* of the definition for 'grace' is not given in the translation. Where are the influence, transformation, and the 'that which causes' parts? These would help clarify the word to mean that the engaging and influential hand of God is removing sin and changing us. In their understanding, the scholars just don't see the need – or don't recognize the significance – of the root word here. And it happens. But let me make this point: You too may come to a place in your understanding, where after you have studied several things and now 'know' something – that you will still be unable to connect all the dots. The accumulation of knowledge is admirable – but you will always need the revelation of God to put all the pieces together correctly. I'll give you that one for free.

About forgiveness, Acts 10:43 states that, "Everyone who believes in Him has received forgiveness of sins." Now, if I've done my job right, you realize that believing in Jesus involves hearing and trusting His voice. Therefore, the only way to be forgiven – which includes the deliverance from your tendency to sin – is through trusting what He speaks to you. Then, if you are really trusting, you will obey Him. This obedience, which has come to you from God's voice, is how He grants you repentance that leads you to the knowledge of the truth (II Timothy 2:25). As you turn and trust, you are given a "repentance for forgiveness of sins" (Luke 24:47).

This removal of our self-choice by trust is further illustrated by Acts 15:9, where it says that God "cleanses their hearts by faith." If you want your heart to be cleansed by God, you must do it His way. When He speaks to you, He will tell you what needs to change in your heart. Be it a dream, vision – or word from God in some other form – God is very good at revealing the true motives of our hearts. Therefore, God does not overlook our sin or merely cover it up – He reveals it so He can cleanse and remove the sin from our hearts. And He does this in relationship with us because we are listening and trusting His influence.

In I John 1:7, it says that "The blood of Jesus cleanses us from all sin." Note: *all* not some. Nothing but God will hold sway over the hearts of true believers when they are cleansed from the dominion of sin. Jesus' blood doesn't merely cover you or somehow mask your transgressions – it deeply cleanses you. This is how you can be changed by God to the point that you love

God with all your heart. The old things that controlled the heart are removed, and new life is given in its place (II Corinthians 5:17).

Terms like salvation, deliverance, forgiveness, repentance, and cleansed are all just different expressions that God uses to teach us the way to be set free from the bondage of sin and self. When we are set free and genuinely different, we cease to practice sin. II Timothy 2:19 declares, "Everyone who confesses the name of the Lord must turn away from wickedness" (NIV). This means you must 'go there.' What I mean is that when God speaks to you a truth – don't just ponder the idea a touch then go back to your ways – no, *go there*. Get to the root of what God is revealing to you. Don't stop seeking until you have the answer. Then repent. Let Him literally change your mind about it. Turn from the thing God shows you is separating you from Him. No matter how many things He tells you – repent. Develop a relationship with God where you can hear Him whisper, and you obey. The wickedness you will turn from has no real value, and you will be the better for it.

Now, I am fully aware that this is not the Christianity that most people are led to believe. Millions of religious people claim salvation and even plead the blood of Jesus while they make their way to hell. They 'believe' the fact that Jesus died on the cross for them and rose from the dead; they 'believe' that they are sinners and are separated from God; and they 'believe' that they have 'given Jesus their lives.' So, in their lack of trust they 'believe' that they are now saved from sin and hell and will be going to heaven. But of what value is any of this if they have not been truly delivered from themselves? Of what significance is their walk with God if they don't walk with God, but self? And of what consequence is there to claiming to be set free from sin if they are still chained to the tendency of that same sin? Can a person purport a relationship with Jesus yet refuse to hear His voice and follow His truth? No. Sin still separates that person from God. All this becomes nothing more than a cross-less, religious game.

The significance of the cross is more than a great 'Jesus salvation story' to acknowledge and live by. The message of the cross is one of the Son hearing the Father, having deep trust in His will, and accomplishing complete obedience with the right heart. That's not to mention the sacrifice of self, the pain of suffering, and the reality of death. Jesus experienced all of these in order to be an example for us to follow. In so doing, He sacrificed Himself by paying the penalty for all sin, and you do not get to have a relationship with Him by making Him a pious pastime. It's just not going to happen. True followers find Jesus when they meet Him at the cross of complete trust and obedience. They find the Savior at the sacrifice of self. Relationship with Christ is found in an exclusive fellowship of sharing in His suffering, and that doesn't change because you want it to. God speaks and tells us to die to ourselves on the cross – and to the Exception it is the smell of life (II Corinthians 2:16).

I Corinthians 1:18 declares, "For the [spoken] word of the cross is to those who are perishing foolishness, but to us who are being saved it is the power of God." Although the cross is truly an enigma to many, dying to self on the cross is in no way a foolish mystery to true seekers. No, the cross is the power – the achieving power[10] – of God. The ability of God to achieve change in us is inherent in the cross and able to deliver us from separation to friendship. When God speaks and influences us to trust Him by crucifying our flesh, the power to die to self and sin is given to us in ample supply. God is more than able to achieve change in our lives and set us free. To whine that it is too hard or too complicated – is a lie – and all liars go to hell (Revelation 21:8). God is able to change your heart, but you must let Him.

You may be asking, "How long is all this dying to self stuff going to take anyway?" Well, that all depends on you. As mentioned before, you will ultimately know that you are right with God when He tells you so – and He's waiting on you. Can it happen instantly? Not really. (Now hang on a minute; give me a chance.) The grace of God has been poured out on you your entire life. 'Instantly' would indicate that you heard God, trusted

His voice, and gave up your life in complete obedience – and all at the exact moment of birth. That would be impressive. So in reality – only God knows how long His influence on you will take. I have known individuals who died to themselves and were delivered in a short time, while others have been hearing God clearly – but not repenting – for years now. The key to finding God is to have a hungry heart. Choose to have a heart that cries out to God – "My soul languishes for Your salvation; I wait for Your [spoken] word" (Psalms 119:81).

The important thing is to trust God and not be in a hurry. Why? First of all, experience. Those who rush, usually have a questionable motive. Quite often they are frantic because they are plagued by the fear of hell. This tends to happen in the middle of the night when their flesh overwhelms them with the thought, 'I have to know I'm okay before I fall asleep.' They are not running to find God; they are running from fear of punishment. Then there are those who agree quickly just to appear spiritual. When this happens, often times the goal is to impress you with the fact that they agree with you. They agree so quickly that they never fully hear or understand what is told to them (I hate it when that happens.) Or maybe the person is just a little too reckless when it comes to perceiving the truth and applying it to his heart. Now, there is nothing wrong with aggressively following God – I encourage it. But to know God requires a person to learn how to take instruction *deeply*. Therefore, in order to better teach this concept, I coined the phrase: Quick to follow, quick to fall.

Let me explain. In Matthew 13:20-21, Jesus was teaching the parable of the sower. He was illustrating how God's spoken word is spread like seed that falls on various places. Well, one of the seeds landed on a rocky surface. The seed grew up quickly, but died just as quick because it had no root. Jesus described it this way:

> *The one on whom seed was sown on the rocky*
> *places, this is the man who hears the word and*
> *immediately receives it with joy; yet he has no*

> *firm root in himself, but is only temporary, and*
> *when affliction or persecution arises because of*
> *the word, immediately he falls away.*

It is important to hear what God speaks. But you must let it root in your heart and become part of you. Otherwise, when affliction arises because of what God speaks to you, there will be little for you to stand on. As quickly as you determined to follow, you will quit. Proverbs 20:21 emphasizes that, "An inheritance gained hurriedly at the beginning will not be blessed in the end." Therefore, be thorough and honest in your quest to love God with all your heart. He is trustworthy to deliver the Exceptions who are willing to go deep, and will be faithful to claim them as His own. Then, when the heat is turned up and so many others retreat in compromise – you will stand.

Now, I realize that there may be some who read this book who are religious in some way and likely under the opinion that they are already saved. I also realize that much of what I discuss will cause you to question your relationship with God. And it is my sincere desire that you do so. That being said, there are countless, undelivered ministers who will urge you – against both Scripture and the Spirit of God – to never question your salvation. This false doctrine causes many who are actually being influenced *by God* to ignore His voice altogether for fear that they will lose a salvation that they don't really have in the first place. Believe me when I tell you that these counterfeit shepherds will answer to God for their deception. The Apostle Paul tells you – as do I – to "Test yourselves to see if you are in the faith; examine yourselves!" (II Corinthians 13:5). Are you really trusting the Living God – His way? Be sure when you seek Him in this that you don't presume. Don't trust what *you* think. Otherwise, your trust in your own understanding will certainly be condemned on that day as well. Hear and trust God.

If you truly desire to be set free from the dominion and control of sin and self, God will give you the wisdom that leads to salvation (II Timothy 3:15). His deliverance is near those who fear Him (Psalms 85:9) and is given to those who turn to Him

(Isaiah 45:22). I pray your heart cries out in earnest, "I am Yours, save me" (Psalms 119:94).

Salvation – Part III
LIVING DELIVERANCE

The idea of salvation and following God has been compared to that of running a race (I Corinthians 9:24). As you would imagine, the start of such a race is critical since an error at the beginning could disqualify you long before you reach the finish line. If recognizing the influence of God and learning to hear His voice is what gets you up to the starting line, then to actually trust in complete obedience is what starts you down the course. But once you are running your race, the next concern – largely overlooked by the religious – is *how* you run that race. I Corinthians 9:24 urges us to "run in such a way as to get the prize" (NIV). Therefore, the prize of a trust relationship with God only comes to those who continue to walk the path of deliverance.

To claim deliverance is one thing, but to live deliverance is something else altogether. Salvation is more than just a one-time decision; it is a lifetime resolution. Most quasi-spiritual people experience a momentary spiritual epiphany, devote a portion of their lives to God, and then back it all up with a lifetime of religious awareness. They support their 'decision' by an occasional glance to the many personal, false doctrines that provide them with a sense of security. But these half-truths only produce an ongoing separation from God by continuing the bondage to a lifestyle of sin. Do you think it is for no reason that Jesus said in John 10:27 that His sheep hear His voice and *follow* Him – or in Luke 9:23 to take up your cross *daily*? Giving your life to Christ must *actually* involve giving your entire life – every moment – to Christ. This is what it means to live out the 'commitment' to Christ so earnestly promised at the beginning of the race.

Far too many denominations teach salvation by categorizing words to excuse the unsaved lifestyle of their congregants. Grace is watered down and labeled as 'saving grace,' as if there were a distinction in the concept. There is not. The grace that "brings salvation" in Titus 2:11 is the same grace that in the very next verse instructs us "to deny ungodliness and worldly desires and to live sensibly, righteously and godly in the present age" (12). The Apostle Paul even includes himself in the reality that grace is currently instructing us all. To inaccurately curtail the influence of God is nothing more than an unregenerate attempt to remove the accountability of the continual changing aspect of grace. God makes His grace available to us, first to be delivered, and then to stay delivered from ourselves every moment of every day. Any half-hearted argument should be resolved by noting that Acts 13:43 simply states, "Continue in the grace of God."

Undelivered theologians try to box in faith the same way with the label 'saving faith.' Once again, if your faith is nothing more than mere doctrinal conformity, it can be limited to avoid the requirement of continuation. But Romans 1:17 testifies that, "The righteous man shall live by faith." *Live* by faith. That means that a person who has been made right with God by hearing, trusting, and obeying His voice – maintains that lifestyle regardless of the doctrines of men.

Once you have taken this matter to heart it will not be surprising when you read "the one who practices righteousness is righteous" but that "the one who practices sin is of the devil" (I John 3:7-8). This shows a stark difference between the person who genuinely gives God his life in every moment and the person who only plays Christianity while still holding on to his sin. Regardless of how you try to water it down or distort it, the fact is "no one born of God practices sin" (I John 3:9).

The truth is that hearing and trusting in the voice of God not only makes us right with Him, but keeps us right with Him. This continual and persistent trust response to God's influence is what it means to walk in repentance. Turning to God in every moment becomes a natural daily heart activity. No longer is the term repentance something to dread or segregate for church on Sunday. Repentance becomes who you are. Hearing, trusting, and obeying God in the moment are the things "that accompany salvation" (Hebrews 6:9) and prove your repentance (Acts 26:20). Having this type of heart is what it means to love God; what it means to die to yourself; what it means to give your life to Jesus.

When you have truly surrendered your life, and He has accepted and delivered you, you will "live on every [spoken] word that proceeds from the mouth of God" (Matthew 4:4). This is your daily bread. It is your sustenance. It is your life. Hearing God in the moment is not a 'have-to' any more than a perfectly prepared meal is drudgery. No, walking out deliverance is joyfulness in relationship to God – especially when every bite of spiritual food causes you to "grow in respect to salvation" (I Peter 2:2). This growth is nurtured by the sustained influence of God until we "become mature, attaining to the whole measure of Christ" (Ephesians 4:13).

Okay, but why would I need to continue to grow in salvation and to mature in deliverance? Because of sin. Let me explain this by using a parable about a field:

> A tenant farmer (you) goes and works in a field (your heart) owned by a Lord (duh☺). It is fraught with weeds and roots and large rocks (sin). The Lord points out to the tenant farmer where to dig out the offending debris (God's voice). The tenant farmer goes to those spots and removes the unwanted items (trust obedience), and the field is soon plowed clean to the Lord's liking (deliverance). Then the tenant farmer takes seed from the Lord (continued voice) and plants it in the field per the Lord's instruction (continued trust obedience). The more the seeds mature and bear fruit (spiritual fruit), the less room for anything else. Now even though the field is completely cleansed and producing fruit, the day-

to-day winds occasionally blow weed seeds (temptation) onto the field (your heart). The Lord tells the farmer where the bad seeds fell (continued influence) and the farmer removes them before they root (continued deliverance). If however, the farmer ignores the Lord and the weeds root (sin), the Lord will reprimand the farmer (rebuke) until the farmer removes the weeds from the field (repentance).

What I find intriguing is that those 'farmers' who fake Christianity want salvation without ever clearing their field. Strangely, they want to be 'saved' into a backslidden state without having to change. But God does not deliver you from sin without delivering you from sin. The debris must be plowed from the field in order to be cultivated. As Jeremiah 4:3 urges, "Break up your unplowed ground and do not sow among thorns" (NIV). The Lord then plants His seed, not yours. And as He desires, the Lord expands your heart 'field' in order to train you to "become transformed into the image of His Son" (Romans 8:29).

Now, when one reads through the New Testament, it becomes quite clear that a true follower of God *can* choose to sin. Although the controlling dominance of sin has been removed – a person is still capable of giving a measure of influence back to the self. As a man is born under the dominion of sin – but influenced by God, so after the kingdom status has changed, a follower is under the dominion of God – but there still exists a sinful outer influence. This evil influence can be likened to a 'seed' of temptation that falls into the heart of a true follower.

It is important to note, however, that being tempted is not sinning. We know this because Jesus was tempted just like us, yet never sinned (Hebrews 4:15). But if a follower allows the seed of desire to grow unchecked, he will be dragged away and enticed to sin (James 1:14-15). Make no mistake, if the excuses that were used to justify sin before following God were not accepted, they will in no way be accepted now. Plus, since a true follower has been freed from the forced control of self and has

God's influence to help him endure (I Corinthians 10:13) – there is even less justification for sin.

That being said, if a true child of God does sin, he has Jesus as an advocate who intercedes on his behalf (I John 2:1). Why do we need an active intercessor? Remember Lucifer and his jealousy toward us? Well, if we sin – Satan is right there to accuse us (Revelation 12:10) by pointing out the nasty truth to God. He tried this with Job (Job 1:11) as well as with Joshua (Zechariah 3:1), and if he can accuse a genuine believer – he will. Jesus stands on the behalf of His children because He intimately knows them (John 10:27) and intimately knows their struggle (Hebrews 4:15). It is because of His desire to keep this intimate relationship with us intact that God also chastises His children. As a matter of fact, God disciplines those He loves and receives (Hebrews 12:6). This correction of a follower reveals the practicality of His intercession, showing how God's grace continually intervenes to bring about change.

Our struggle is caused by the devil, who I like to call 'Old Monkeyfoot' because he craves for an opportunity to get a foothold on your soul (Ephesians 4:27). This should be avoided at all costs. If Satan can gain a foothold by enticing a child of God to be entangled in self again, he will be well pleased. If Satan can convince him to change the grace of God into a license to sin, he will be ecstatic.

Pertaining to a Christian being involved in sin, the Apostle Paul asked, "Shall we go on sinning so that grace may increase?" (Romans 6:1 NIV). His answer was emphatically no. Only a fool would expect an increase in the changing influence of God while he is rejecting and swerving from that very influence. So what's the concern? It's not like a Christian can fall from grace, right? Wrong. Paul dealt with some believers who got caught up in religious sin and told them they were alienated from Christ and had "fallen from grace" (Galatians 5:4). They had fallen out of the influence of God.

So the obvious concern is that a follower who continues to swerve away from God's path can become "subject again to the yoke of slavery" (Galatians 5:1). To turn back to the miserable principles that a Christian has escaped from is to chance "being enslaved all over again" (Galatians 4:9). Now, you can twist these verses any way you want to, but the truth is still the truth. Slavery is slavery. A person who alters the concept of being 'enslaved all over again' into somehow *not* being enslaved – has embraced an invented doctrine of men. An Exception does not distort the meaning of words just because the truth isn't suiting him. Instead, an honest search for the truth by listening to the voice of God initiates a repentance of the preconceived misperception.

Salvation – Part IV
FINISHING DELIVERANCE

Simply stated, once you are actually delivered, you have the right to leave the ancient path. God will never force a person to remain faithful to Him. Hebrews 11:15 says that, "If they had been thinking of that country from which they went out, they would have had opportunity to return." If you love the bondage of Egypt, you may return to it. Ultimately, God will let you reap what you sow – good or bad (Galatians 6:7-8). But just as salvation is a process whereby God influences change, so walking away from Him is a process as well. Proverbs 15:10 states that, "Stern discipline awaits him who leaves the path" (NIV) – demonstrating that the hand of God will redirect a child's missteps. It should be noted that there is a clear difference between those who respect this type of instruction and those who resist – in that "He who heeds discipline shows the way of life, but whoever ignores correction leads others astray" (Proverbs 10:17 NIV). To put it bluntly, "He who hates reproof is stupid" (Proverbs 12:1).

An important question that many will undoubtedly ask is: Will one sin cause a person to lose his salvation? No. To help us out, let's think of the field. Does one weed mean the field is lost and back under the control of the weeds? Of course not. Do two

weeds mean the field has reverted control? No. And the Lord
will be more than diligent to speak and reprove the farmer if the
weeds remain. Well then, at what point do the weeds take control
of the field again? The weeds will take over control when the
farmer stops listening and trusting the Lord. This can happen. To
hold onto a doctrine that pretends the field could never be choked
out by the weeds is not only unscriptural, it is folly.

Case in point, II Peter 2:20 strengthens this concern of
being overcome by sin:

> *For if, after they have escaped the defilements of*
> *the world by the knowledge of the Lord and*
> *Savior Jesus Christ, they are again entangled in*
> *them and are overcome, the last state has become*
> *worse for them than the first.*

To make my point further, let's read this verse in the literal
translation:

> *(20) For if by a full knowledge of the Lord and*
> *Savior, Jesus Christ, they have escaped the*
> *defilements of the world, and again being*
> *entangled they have been overcome by these, then*
> *their last things are worse than the first.*
> *(21) For it was better for them not to have fully*
> *known the way of righteousness, than fully*
> *knowing to turn from the holy commandment*
> *delivered to them.*[11]

The person being discussed in this verse has been
delivered from the world, his salvation secured by a full knowledge
of Christ. If this person becomes entangled with the defilements
of the world *again* – which stresses that he was once entangled
but no more – and if he is overcome by that snarl of sin, he will
be worse off than when he started. The reality is that he fully
knew God. The reality is that he fully knew the way of
righteousness – hearing, trusting, and fully obeying the voice of

God. The reality is that he got caught up in the dominion of self-will all over again – and God says this is worse than never knowing Him in the first place. Now that's a bad day.

But what is a worse state than being in hell? I'll tell you. Imagine being person 'A' in hell. You lived your life the way you wanted to, maybe mixed in some religion just for the fun of it – but never let go of your opinion or your will. You die and as you stand in front of the throne of God you are confronted with the truth. It's not good. Congratulations, you are allowed, per *your* choice, to continue your separation from God for eternity. Yeah, you feel bad, angry, and strangely still justified in your own eyes (that's where the weeping and gnashing of teeth come in), but it was your choice from the beginning. Now imagine being person 'B.' As person 'B,' you lived your life separated from God until one day you recognized that God was speaking to you. You heard and started trusting, letting go of yourself. You kept following His voice until one day God accepted you, adopting you as His own. So then you were delivered from self and had joy and peace in a deep trust relationship with your Father. But after time you became complacent. Maybe you even believed the lie that God was bound to your agreement even though you consistently broke it. You sinned more and more, all the while ignoring God's continued influence for you to walk in repentance. The vines of sin strangled you, and soon you were overcome again by the dominion of sin. Then, you died. Now you stand before the throne of God and are confronted with the truth just like person 'A.' You too are now allowed, per *your* choice, to enter eternity separated from God in hell. The difference is that as you suffer in anger and self-justification – you know a haunting truth. You had found God and had been set free from what brought you here – but you chose to swerve from Him for momentary pleasure. And because of that truth, you are worse off than person 'A.' You will weep bitterly for eternity – and you will weep harder than most.

The fact is that today when a person trusts God and is chosen by Him, God grafts him into Himself. Much like an unnatural limb is grafted onto a tree, so the new follower is delivered from his previous life as a wild branch. Paul points out that the security of that grafted in branch stands solely on faith (Romans 11:20). Please comprehend this truth – *"You stand by your faith"* (20). He then warns against the arrogance that presumes upon salvation even when a lack of trust creeps in. It should be made clear that if God did not spare previous unbelief, He will not spare you either (21). Then to round out the thought he writes, "Behold then the kindness and severity of God; to those who fell, severity, but to you, God's kindness, if you continue in His kindness; otherwise you also will be cut off" (22). Please note: *"if you continue. . ."*

Jesus discussed this with the disciples in John 15:2 when He said that "every branch in Me that does not bear fruit" His Father "takes away." Make no mistake – this is a branch that is *in* Jesus that refuses to continue hearing and trusting to the point of fruit. This is a reminder that only continued, obedient faith is authentic faith. These branches that are taken away are thrown into the fire and burned (6). Therefore Jesus himself warned that once a person is abiding in Him, he would do well to remain there.

For a person to actually lose salvation – to become undelivered again – means that he has willingly renounced ownership of his relationship with God. The relationship of trusting the voice of God is abandoned in order to regain the self and its affections. II Timothy 2:12 states plainly, "If we disown Him, He will disown us" (NIV). The 'us' makes it clear that not only was Paul including Timothy in this warning, but himself as well. I pray you are able to perceive the value of the warning, "Take care, brethren, that there not be in any one of you an evil, unbelieving heart that falls away from the Living God" (Hebrews 3:12).

If this process of walking away from relationship continues, it does so under the discipline of God. After repeated attempts to rein you in and draw you back to repentance, God will eventually let you go your way. The process of leaving Him is allowed to end. In Hebrews 6:4-5, it refers to people "who have once been enlightened and have tasted the heavenly gift and have been made partakers of the Holy Spirit, and have tasted the good [spoken] word of God." Needless to say, the people of Hebrews 6:4-5 are followers of God. Then verse 6 explains what happens to those who have been enlightened should they become fallen away. The sad result of their rebellion is that it will be "impossible to be brought back to repentance, since they again crucify to themselves the Son of God and put Him to open shame." Understand that once this level of rejection has taken place, turning back to God will no longer be an option.

Let's take the concept of falling away deeper. The word for "fallen away," in the Greek, means to fall away or fall aside – denoting abandonment. The word indicates no error of weakness or accident, but signifies a deliberate act of sin.[12] Dr. James Strong defines this concept of abandonment as – to apostatize[13] – which is a total renunciation of allegiance to God. However you choose to consider it, the concept of falling away is such a serious abandonment of God that the person so doing will not be granted repentance ever again (6). Once sin has entangled a believer's soul to this point, the believer ceases to believe and repent, thereby abandoning relationship with God. Upon this disowning of all things genuinely spiritual, God lets you go.

Why aren't they allowed to come back to repentance? Well, because the Scripture says that, "If we go on sinning willfully after receiving the knowledge of the truth, there no longer remains a sacrifice for sins" (Hebrews 10:26). This is supported by the fact that I Peter 3:18 maintains that Christ died for sins "once for all." Therefore, to be brought back to repentance after apostasy would require Jesus to die all over again and subject Him to open shame, and that's just not going to happen. As a matter of fact, the only thing left for the person who knows the truth but deliberately lives in sin is "a terrifying expectation of judgment and the fury of fire which will consume the adversaries" (Hebrews 10:27).

The parable in Hebrews 6:7-8 reinforces the reason for such expectation by explaining:

Ground that drinks the rain which often falls on it
and brings forth vegetation useful to those for
whose sake it is also tilled, receives a blessing
from God; but if it yields thorns and thistles, it is
worthless and close to being cursed, and it ends
up being burned.

This is land that has been cleared and tilled. Time and care have been given in hopes it would produce fruit. Yet it refuses to bear fruit regardless of the amount of rain poured upon it. All that work wasted. Of what value is such land? It is only good for burning. Thus a heart that has been cleared and tilled, but then rejects the continued influence of God poured out upon it – proves worthless as well. Producing thorns instead of fruit is to mock God and to take His grace for granted. This heart is overrun by sin because it didn't continue in God – and now it never will.

In Revelation 2:4-5, Jesus gave warning to the believers at the church in Ephesus. He told them, "You have left your first love. Therefore remember from where you have fallen, and repent and do the deeds you did at first or else I am coming to you and will remove your lamp stand out of its place – unless you repent." Slice it how you want, but 'remove your lamp stand' was not a decorating tip. As we have seen in the verses we have previously studied, God does not play around if you continually reject His voice. This is seen even more dramatically in Revelation 2:16 when Jesus told the people in Pergamum to repent or else He was going to come to them and "make war against them with the sword of [His] mouth." He told them to repent or become an enemy, and there is no way an enemy of God will inherit the kingdom.

Wouldn't it be horrifying to stand before God on that day and have to answer for the fact that after you were saved from Satan's grasp and experienced deliverance under God's rule, that you reneged on the deal by deciding that Satan's rule was better? Talk about backing the wrong horse. I cannot imagine the wrath in store for those who realign themselves as the enemies of God.

No wonder the Bible exhorts us to "work out your salvation with fear and trembling" (Philippians 2:12). It makes it easy to recognize the need to strengthen the disciples by "encouraging them to continue in the faith" (Acts 14:22). As Hebrews 10:31 declares, "It is a terrifying thing to fall into the hands of the Living God."

The question is not at all about God's ability to keep those entrusted to Him. In John 10:28, Jesus makes it clear that "no one will snatch them out of My hand." The Greek word for 'snatch' is *harpazo*, to seize upon with force – to rob.[14] Simply put, no one is able to forcibly steal a genuine Christian away from God. Your security stands on faith – and that is between you and God. The problem, as we have seen, is the continuation of that faith. If you choose to stop trusting His voice, God will reluctantly let you walk away from His hand. I Timothy 4:1 indicates that, "The Spirit clearly says that in later times some will abandon the faith" (NIV). To 'abandon' is to withdraw, remove oneself, forsake, desert, cease from something.[15] These words mean just what they imply. To withdraw from faith you would have to be *at faith*, to forsake faith you must *have faith*, and to cease from faith you would have to be *actively faithing*. God will never take salvation away from a follower; deliverance is lost when the follower chooses to forsake God.

Let's make a couple things clear. I do believe in the security of the believer. It's just that I believe in the security of the *believer*. Stop trusting, there is no security – only a fearful expectation etc. etc. Yes, I believe once saved always saved. I believe once saved always saved – *if* – the person continues to trust God.

"Well, I don't like your doctrine because I don't like not knowing if I'm going to heaven or not." Where have *you* been? A trust relationship is not fraught with frantic wondering. If you don't know whether or not you are going to heaven, it is because God has not told you so and apparently you are going to hell. But you *can* know. You can know for certain not only about heaven, but about every detail of your walk with God. You will know for certain when God tells you so. This is the only way to have true hope – not just 'hope so.'

I have even heard the parental argument that once a child of God, always a child of God – no matter what it can never change. First of all, parents disown and disinherit their children quite often, so there goes that argument. Secondly – and I hate to be the one to tell you this but – you're adopted. It's true, don't cry, your Father still loves you very much. A worldly child that God has *truly* delivered is adopted into His family (Romans 8:15-17). The reality is that you were an ugly baby left on the doorstep of this world. Lost, naked, and hungry. The Father found you, pitied you, and went about drawing you to Himself. Given that you eventually submitted yourself to Him by becoming a genuine disciple – He clothed you, fed you, and then adopted you as His own. And *even then*, as an adopted child we are to be responsible to persevere (Romans 8:23, 25).

Then there are those who will argue that Romans 11:29 proves that salvation can't be lost because the gifts of God are "irrevocable." Really? Irrevocable in that they cannot be recalled, undone, or altered[16] like in Webster's Dictionary? Is that what this word really means? Hmmm. Let's take a look at that dusty Greek dictionary again. Here it is, irrevocable, Strong's number 278 – *ametameletos*.[17] It comes from two words, *a*, without and 3338 *metamelomai*, to change one's mind, to regret.[18] So really, an unbiased and untainted definition is "the gifts of God are without regret." That is a far cry from irrevocable, don't you think? (Who translates these verses, really?) Hey, do you want to get real mean and nasty? The word for 'gift' is one we have looked at before, meaning – the result of changing influence.[19] So humor me in this – there are large groups of people who base their doctrine of once saved always saved on a verse that really reads – the results of the changing influence of God are without regret? Wow, that's got to sting.

Most people who argue against the truth that a Christian must continue, do so for one of two reasons: One – they are simply ignorant of the truth and have chosen a deception that seems right in their own eyes, or two – they are protecting a lifestyle of justified self-will in hidden rebellion against God.

Either way, the truth was never sought out. Honestly, if you choose to ignore the reality of these verses that are being unveiled for you – you have a much bigger problem and need to find God.

It may help your overall understanding if we observe how Paul lived out his relationship with God in view of these issues. In Philippians 3:11, Paul desires to "attain to the resurrection of the dead." What he is saying is that he wants to be changed on that day and live with God eternally. Then in the following verse, he makes this statement – "Not that I have already obtained it or have already become perfect. . ." (12). Wait a minute, Paul's saved, isn't he? Yes. Then he has already obtained deliverance, right? Well, yes and no. Yes, he has been changed and accepted by God and has the promise of eternal life – but no, in that Paul knows the truth that there is a much fuller, more complete salvation waiting for him – if he continues. I Peter 1:5-6 testifies that followers "are protected by the power of God through faith for a salvation ready to be revealed in the last time." Paul knew that his *final* salvation was protected by his *continued* salvation – his *continued* trust in the voice of God.

In Philippians 3:12, Paul continued to say, "I press on to take hold of that for which Christ Jesus took hold of me" (NIV). And what pray tell was that? What did Jesus take hold of Paul for? For a complete and eternal deliverance in relationship with God. Paul goes on to say, "Brethren, I do not regard myself as having laid hold of it yet" (13) but "I press on toward the goal for the prize of the upward call of God in Christ Jesus" (14). The Apostle held in his heart the truth that he must continue and knew that if he did – the prize of eternal relationship would be secured. Next he makes a plea to those who read his letter by writing that they should "have this attitude; and if in anything you have a different attitude, God will reveal that also to you" (15).

Paul proved he was an Exception. So, I encourage you to have the same attitude as he did when he said, "I run in such a way, as not without aim . . . so that, after I have preached to others, I myself will not be disqualified" (I Corinthians 9:26-27).

I tell you the truth, if Paul could be disqualified, so could you. Aim toward God. Turn your ear to His voice. There is no need to perish, struggle, or backslide. When God speaks, listen. When He corrects you, learn from Him. And if God rebukes you, it is a good thing – repent. As God told me once in a dream, "Be quick to repent and humble of heart." Grow to understand the deep security of a believer who continues to believe.

I urge you to start, run, and finish the race hand in hand with God. Know for yourself where the starting line is. Know for sure how to run. And know for certain that you will cross the finish line in relationship with God. The Father will give you all the grace you need to "persevere so that when you have done the will of God, you will receive what He has promised" (Hebrews 10:36 NIV). That is why we are told to "lay aside every encumbrance and the sin which so easily entangles us, and let us run with endurance the race that is set before us" (Hebrews 12:1). Remember, "The one who endures to the end, he shall be saved" (Matthew 24:13).

Application Summary

There is a meaning to this thing we call life. Death. Spiritual life only springs from death. Your old nature must die in order for a new you to emerge. But the battle for freedom from your old self is part of a much bigger picture, a much larger conflict. God created you and desires to deliver you for His glory in order to put His enemies to shame.

God is not saving you to keep you out of hell, so that should not be your motive. God is also not delivering you to get you into heaven, so *that* should not be your motive. God is delivering you so you will let go of your trust relationship with yourself – and exchange it for a deep, trust relationship with Him. This salvation is a very real deliverance from self and sin. To be delivered for real, you will have to stop sinning and stop going your own way. This is death to opinion, likes, and dislikes. This is death to offense, bitterness, and justification. This is death to all things 'you.' The only way to know what to die to is found in the leadership of God. His voice will guide you and give you the strength to follow through to repentance.

Trusting in what you 'do' is to trust the work of man, the arm of man. Therefore, to place your *faith* on the fact that you *prayed* and *you received* Jesus sets your soul on a course to hell. Your trust should never be in something you 'did.' If your faith is in a work or anything other than His voice, you are deceived. There is little value in accepting Jesus unless He accepts you. So receive Jesus, but do it His way – let His voice draw you to Himself as you surrender everything He asks of you. Many are called to follow, but only a few are chosen and adopted as His children.

The wage you will earn for choosing to swerve and miss God is spiritual death, but the result of God's changing influence on you is eternal life in relationship with God. Therefore, let go of the self-choice in your heart. Let God forgive you – remove the sin – and let His blood cleanse you for real. No rose-colored glasses will hide your sin from His sight. All things are laid bare before God, and you *will* give an account.

When God speaks about an area of your heart, go there. If He is speaking symbolically, go deep with Him and learn His language. Meditate on the word of God to you and seek with all you know. He *will* reveal the truth to you – if – you'll go there.

Jesus died as a sacrifice to pay the penalty for your sin. But He also died as an example to instruct you how to die to your self. Meet Him there – at the cross. Meet Him in heart, to willingly lay down all you know before His feet. Then take up your cross and follow Him daily. God will forgive your self-will, cleanse your heart, break the dominion of the sin in your life, and change you.

Run in such a way as to win the race, not just to look good religiously or to be okay. Cease to sin by practicing righteousness. Live by faith, trusting in God's spoken word to you. These are the things that accompany salvation. Continue to walk out repentance by hearing and trusting God's voice to complete obedience. Learn to live on every word that comes from

His mouth. They are life to you and will transform you into His image.

Once you have been truly saved, Old Monkeyfoot will furiously desire to get a foothold on your heart, and will work to entangle you in sin and self all over again. Satan desires to see you subjected again to your previous slavery. If he can gain your heart again, then you will be his forever.

Once on the path, you may take the opportunity to leave it – but know that God will show you His love by disciplining you. Be comforted by the stern discipline that awaits you because it is not His desire to lose that relationship. Maybe not one sin or two, but eventually, if you continue to walk away from God, you will be overcome again by the dominion of sin. After this abandonment, you will not be allowed to return to repentance. Jesus died once for all, and He will not do it again for those who, after having been under His rule, choose to reject Him and become His enemy. Hell will be worse for those who commit apostasy. Therefore, work out your deliverance with a healthy fear and let your heart tremble before the Lord of the Universe.

God does not regret the changes He has influenced in your life – it's been worth the effort. However, don't take deliverance for granted. Once you are saved, there is only a fearful expectation if you leave the path. But know this; no one can steal you away from God. He is firm in His grasp. He will, however, allow you to leave of your own volition, so understand the reality that there is security for the believer provided you stay a believer – continuing to trust in God. And once you *have been* delivered, you can absolutely stay delivered – if you continue to walk in that deliverance.

True followers are protected by the power of God for a salvation to be revealed on that day – on the condition that they continue in faith. Those who have the heart to endure to the end will be the ones who are ultimately delivered for eternity. And if in anything you have a different attitude, may God reveal these truths to you so that you may repent and find a salvation that is genuine, certain, and eternal.

Challenging Your Perception

1. True salvation is more than just feeling okay, it is to be delivered from the practice of daily sin that chooses to swerve toward the self – but do you have eyes to see it?

2. Do you excuse your fleshly behavior instead of letting God deliver you? Do you find within yourself a desire to be truly delivered, or are you content to stay the way you are?

3. Are you willing to repent, holding nothing back from God? Or, when you stand before God on that day, what excuse will you give for your separation because of your daily sin?

Endnotes

1. James Strong, LL.D., S.T.D., *The New Strong's Exhaustive Concordance of the Bible*, Dictionary of the Hebrew Bible, copyright 1990 by Thomas Nelson Publishers, page 32, Hebrew #1966, *hay-lale*.
2. Spiros Zodhiates, TH.D., *The Complete Word Study Dictionary New Testament*, D/B/A AMG Publishers, copyright 1992 by Spiros Zodhiates and AMG International Inc., page 1360, Greek #4991, *soteria*.
3. Ibid., page 1353, Greek #4982, *sozo*.
4. Ibid., page 1471, Greek #5486, *charisma*.
5. Ibid., page 1471, Greek #5486, *–ma*.
6. Ibid., page 233, Greek #630, *apoluo*.
7. Ibid., page 299, Greek # 863, *aphiemi*.
8. Zodhiates and AMG International Inc., page 485, Greek #1411, *dunamis*.
9. Jay P. Green, *The Interlinear Bible*, Hendrickson Publishers, copyright Second Edition 1986 Jay P. Green, and side column – *A Literal Translation of the Bible*, copyright 1985 Jay P. Green, page 944.
10. Spiros Zodhiates, TH.D., *The Complete Word Study Dictionary New Testament*, D/B/A AMG Publishers, copyright 1992 by Spiros

Zodhiates and AMG International Inc., page 1112, Greek #3895, *parapesoumai.*

11. James Strong, LL.D., S.T.D., *The New Strong's Exhaustive Concordance of the Bible*, Dictionary of the Greek Testament, copyright 1990 by Thomas Nelson Publishers, page 55, Greek #3895, *parapesoumai.*

12. Spiros Zodhiates, TH.D., *The Complete Word Study Dictionary New Testament*, D/B/A AMG Publishers, copyright 1992 by Spiros Zodhiates and AMG International Inc., page 257, Greek #726, *harpazo.*

13. Ibid., page 301, Greek #868, *aphistemi.*

14. Webster's New World College Dictionary, Fourth Edition, Macmillan USA, copyright 1999, page 756.

15. Spiros Zodhiates, TH.D., *The Complete Word Study Dictionary New Testament*, D/B/A AMG Publishers, copyright 1992 by Spiros Zodhiates and AMG International Inc., page 133, Greek #278, *ametameletos.*

16. Ibid., page 968, Greek #3338, *metamelomai.*

17. Ibid., page 1471, Greek #5486, *charisma.*

The Church must not be looked for where man is, but where God is.

Eberhard Arnold

Let them boldly assert the cause of Christ in an age when so many that bear the name of Christian are ashamed of Him.

William Wilberforce

Untruthfulness destroys fellowship, but truth cuts false fellowship.

Dietrich Bonhoeffer

God alone matters here.

Eberhard Arnold

Chapter
9

AN UNCOMMON COMMUNITY
(The Undeniable Difference)

"And the Lord their God will save them in that day as the flock of His people;
For they are as the stones of a crown, sparkling in His land."
Zechariah 9:16

After the excitement of his miraculous recovery, our hero turns to view the grand feast prepared by the villagers. And what a feast it is. Around what appears to be a common community area are hundreds of different meals set out for all to partake. He sees dozens of main courses filled with hearty cuts of beef, succulent side dishes, and desserts that could make any mouth water. There is even a large hog on a spit over a fire that fills the air with the smell of a thousand afternoon barbecues. The hero is encouraged to sit down and eat, which he does gladly.

As captivating as the food in front of him is, there is something that starts to stand out in the hero's mind. The people. Amid the reality of guns, threats, and bad guy zapping magical beams – they remain calm, cool, and completely collected. As a matter of fact, they seem downright enthusiastic about the entire event. He listens as the villagers swap details of the incident, each sharing their individual thoughts and perceptions. The older people help instruct the understanding of the younger children, who seem quite eager to learn.

Throughout the feast, he can't help but notice the villager's overwhelming joyfulness, contented simplicity, and sincere concern for each other. And not the typical, shallow empathy he had seen half-heartedly displayed time and again back in society – but a deep, genuine honesty with each other. As the sun slowly goes down and the campfire songs begin to mix with the sounds of the night, the hero is stunned by just how different these people are.

ભ્ર૪૭ાબૂભ્ર૪૭ાબૂભ્ર૪૭ાબૂભ્ર૪૭ાબૂભ્ર૪૭ાબૂભ્ર૪૭ાબૂ

Different. The *true* church is different. It is definitively uncommon, atypical, and out of the ordinary. As different as the true church is from the world, so a true body of Christ is from every other church imitation advertising itself as the real thing. Unlike so many counterfeit churches that court popularity under the guise of ministry, the family of Jesus desires no such attraction and plays no such game. New trendy programs are as despised as lifeless traditions are detested. The goal of such a true fellowship does not consist of developing children and youth ministries in order to attract religious families; create college coffee shops in order to be the hip church in town; or to develop a 'social gospel' cause in an attempt to justify its existence and to give the impression that it cares about the community. To turn God's family into a church growth formula is simply unacceptable. No, the valid goal of a true church is to follow God with *all* its heart and to teach the Exceptions to do the same.

The main factor that makes the true church an uncommon community is the manifestation of God in His people. Unlike a false fellowship that fabricates an artificial presence of God through hype, borrowed doctrines, and the presumption of positive confession – genuine followers have within them a changed spirit and a relationship with the Father not based on wishful thinking. Since they have *fully* surrendered to God and have been made right with God *His* way, they meet together to experience Him – "For where two or three have gathered together in My name, I am there in their midst" (Matthew 18:20). The presence of God, now inherent in their hearts, is compounded by the relationship with other truly saved individuals.

Don't be easily fooled; this fellowship is in no way based upon shared aptitudes, mutual aversions, or common financial brackets. Not a single person joins because the church makes him feel comfortable or because he prefers the music. Followers unite with a community of genuine believers because God told them to, and they meet as family because they all have God as their Father (II Corinthians 6:18).

And this is no dysfunctional family. As true children, they have a lifestyle of agreeing with God *and* each other. Did you catch that? The common thread of this uncommon community is to be of one heart and of one mind (Acts 4:32, Philippians 1:27) – all in agreement with the will of God. How can this be? They all practice righteousness.

Every true believer lives and breathes righteousness – hearing and trusting the voice of God in obedience. It is "by this the children of God and the children of the devil are obvious: anyone who does not practice righteousness is not of God" (I John 3:10). This reality of relationship serves to differentiate true children of God from every other impersonation. God's children are His possession, and He creates a spirit in them so different that "you will again distinguish between the righteous and the wicked, between one who serves God and one who does not serve Him" (Malachi 3:18).

These uncommon people live out more than just the stereotypical religious experience. Although they may participate in the above average spirituality of prayer meetings, Bible study, and non-liturgical worship – they do not consider them the end all. And as valuable as it may be to have an hour of quiet time for God each morning, these true believers refuse to box their relationship with God into such short religious moments. Rather, they have learned to actively "pray without ceasing"

(I Thessalonians 5:17). From the second they awake, to the moment they fall asleep, these believers are able to stay in constant communication with their Father. This is much more than a head bowed, hand clasped, pious, religious exercise – it is an openness – where every thought is willingly laid bare before God. Every contemplation, reflection, and notion is given willingly to Him. No idea, concept, or opinion is ever guarded, pretended, or hidden. Just a blatant honesty of all things set before His presence. Relationship in real-time.

This real-time relationship is a persistent following of God and is proof that the believer belongs to the Father. Romans 8:14 explains, "For all who are being led by the Spirit of God, these are sons of God." The goal of these children is not to pursue their own self-will, but to pursue the will of God – and to do so in every moment. Though actively living in the world, they refuse to be conformed to it (or any religious adaptation thereof) and are thus "transformed by the renewing of [their] mind" (Romans 12:2). In this way, they are able to follow the Spirit and "prove what the will of God is" (2), regardless of their location or endeavor.

To possess this revelation from God is a foundational indicator of the true church. The depth of this reality is found in Matthew 16 when Peter confessed that Jesus was the Christ, the Son of the Living God. After his confession, Jesus said to him, "Blessed are you, Simon Barjona, because flesh and blood did not reveal this to you, but My Father who is in heaven" (Matthew 16:17). It was then that Jesus spoke something so often misinterpreted that it makes my head spin. He told Peter, who was obviously called Simon at the time, "You are Peter, and on this rock I will build my church" (18). Now, in order to make sense of this verse, let's look at a couple of words. First, the word for 'Peter' is *petros*, a stone, a piece or fragment of a rock.[1] Then the word for 'rock' means a mass of rock,[2] a projecting rock or cliff.[3] So we have two differing concepts: one is a small movable type of stone, while the other is a large mass of bedrock. So let's put it all together:

Blessed are you Simon Barjona, because flesh and
blood did not reveal this to you, but My Father
who is in heaven. I also say to you that you are a
small piece of rock, and on this large mass of rock
I will build My church.
Matthew 16:17-18

So what is the large, massive rock that Jesus is talking of? Well, it clearly is not the small movable Peter. Some would say that Jesus is referring to Himself, and I would agree with that argument since He is the rejected "Stumbling Stone" and "Rock of Offense" (I Peter 2:7-8). But I believe Jesus is also referring to something else, something deeper. The answer is found there in the context of the verse right before it: Peter received revelation from God. Jesus is stating that the uncommon community of His body will be built upon the fact that God *reveals* the truth – the revelation of a relationship with Christ – to His children. This bedrock of the Father speaking and revealing Christ – and our coming into agreement with Him – is the very foundation of His people. The basis of the ancient path is grounded on the reality that God makes Himself known to those who will hear – to those like Peter willing to be moved. And unlike a flesh and blood understanding that follows God only in pretense – true revelation from the Father is dependable, solid, and trustworthy. So solid is the foundation of God speaking and revealing His will to us that "the gates of hades will not overpower it" (Matthew 16:18).

The gates of hell do not fear religion, or liturgy; demons do not cower before saber rattling and bravado; and Lucifer is not the least bit threatened by a church that has built a temple to itself just outside the narrow gate boasting a non-existent relationship with God. The legions of hell do, however, fear one individual willing to hear and trust God in complete obedience. Why? A righteous child carries within his heart an ear to hear the authoritative will of the Father. I John 5:14 states, "This is the confidence which we have before Him that, if we ask anything according to His will He hears us." And then the next verse is one that can shake the very gates of hell – "And if we know that

He hears us in whatever we ask, we know that we have the requests which we have asked from Him" (15).

Now I hope you are able to catch the reality of this truth. When one follower of God hears and trusts the revelation of His will, God hears and grants their request – because they are serving *His* interest, *His* desire. Well, doesn't God hear everyone's request? No, not according to Psalms 66:18 which declares, "If I regard wickedness in my heart, the Lord will not hear." If you are swerving from God and ignoring His will, why would He pay attention to your selfish desires? God just won't listen, and rightfully so. But, one person in agreement with God can be used by Him to enact His will on earth just as it is in heaven. When a true child prays the will of God – God hears agreement. That's when Satan's kingdom here on earth will be seriously threatened. And that's just from one follower who agrees with God.

Now, imagine what can happen when many true believers meet together as one. When God establishes a community that is of one heart and one mind with Him, its members walk in the light of God's revelation and are able to know what pleases Him (Ephesians 5:8). This insight into the truth of the Father is what causes the authentic church to shine (Daniel 12:3), and that light will draw and illuminate others (Isaiah 60:3). When these followers lead others to the righteousness that they themselves experience with God, it will cause them to shine even greater (Daniel 12:3).

The Community of God is therefore lighting the way for other Exceptions, yet clearly in an uncommon way. Rather than ignoring the lost by a performance of lip service, or by fleshly telling anyone in ear shot their testimony – true children choose rather to hear and obey God. I know, what a radical concept, but the only truly effective one there is. There is only one way to know which individual God is actively drawing – and that is to be led by the Spirit of God who knows. Otherwise, it is a grand waste of time, energy, and resources. The people of a genuine fellowship of God did not come to God by following the flesh, so they will not incorporate the arm of man in leading others there, either.

Please understand that true evangelistic enthusiasm is produced by God's leadership and not by guilt or shame. No longer does a person go across the street and try to lead his neighbor in an unscriptural prayer just because the preacher laid a guilt trip on him Sunday morning. God's sheep hear and follow *His* voice, not man's manipulation.

The process an uncommon community uses to lead the Exceptions to Jesus is found in Matthew 28:19-20:

> *Go therefore and make disciples of all the nations,*
> *baptizing them in the name of the Father and the*
> *Son and the Holy Spirit, teaching them to observe*
> *all that I commanded you.*

First let me remark on the word 'go.' The Greek word is *poreumai*, meaning to transport oneself,[4] to traverse or travel.[5] Once you apply the parsing, the full meaning of the word is 'as you have traveled.' What's my point? Preachers constantly proclaim that Jesus commanded us to go. He did not. He commanded us *to make disciples* – and we are responsible to make those disciples as we live and traverse this earth. If God wants you to go someplace specific, He is more than capable to speak and tell you so. But to arbitrarily go out as you see fit and call it 'evangelism' or 'missions' is to refuse the leadership of His Spirit. To reject this reality is to act as the Pharisees who traveled far and wide in order to make one proselyte "twice as much a son of hell" as they were (Matthew 23:15).

All evangelistic efforts of a true community of Christ are determined by the head of the church. Since Christ is the head of the body (Colossians 1:18), it is Christ who speaks and leads His children to the appropriate field of harvest. It is then that a genuine fellowship "bears fruit that will last" (John 15:16 NIV) by instructing new disciples to follow *all that the Lord commands.*

Next, I would like you to note the order that the verse is written: "make disciples . . . baptizing them." Counterfeit ministries reverse this sequence by baptizing individuals who have prayed a prayer, and then putting them through a six-week discipleship survival course in hopes that the whole thing sticks. Although this is status quo in most of Christendom, it is not Christian. Jesus commanded His children to teach and instruct[6] new followers – making them true disciples – *then* to baptize them into the community of believers.

Once a true disciple, the new follower has chosen God over his possessions (Luke 14:33), has chosen the leadership of the Holy Spirit over his family (Matthew 10:37), and has chosen the lordship of Christ over himself (Luke 14:26). The person has become a disciple, disciplined by the voice of God, proving that he is not illegitimate (Hebrews 12:8). This is so much more than a momentary decision or an acceptance of a doctrinal mindset. Discipleship is a complete surrendering of one's heart and soul in relationship to the guiding voice of God, and once the person is fully immersed in God – only then is he immersed in water.

Now any good Bible scholar will notice that early in the book of Acts the disciples baptized much quicker than this. But an even better Bible scholar will point out that after problems arose of false believers infiltrating the church (I John 2:19, Acts 15:1, I Corinthians 5:11, Titus 1:10, 16), things had to change. The final doctrinal stance of Paul in Acts 26:20 matched the first position of John the Baptist in Matthew 3:8 – first prove your repentance by your deeds. In an uncommon community, it is only these 'disciples' who are to be baptized.

This concern about false believers caused the early church to cling all the more to the requirement of complete repentance before baptism. Justin, an evangelist who was martyred in 165 AD, put it plainly – "Only he who has truly ceased to sin shall receive baptism."[7] In order to properly oversee this responsibility, individuals were taught as 'hearers' and then observed to see if their lifestyle backed up their profession. Only after they had ceased to sin and given ample proof of conversion were they baptized and allowed to join the community of believers.[8]

These new followers plunged their lives so deeply into Christ that the baptismal waters became a symbol of the cleansing blood of Jesus. Each one who willingly took this 'military oath' of baptism broke with the status quo of society and committed themselves to live and die for the cross.[9] This ancient path of commitment to God, though concealed by generations of non-Christian Christianity, is the path that a true community of Christ travels upon.

After these 'hearers' became 'doers' of the spoken word, they were welcomed into the body with the Meal of Fellowship. Known also as Communion or the Meal of Thanksgiving, it was fashioned after the last supper of the Lord where the food eaten represented His body and the drink represented His blood. The Meal of the first church was therefore more like an ordinary mealtime than a religious ritual.[10] Generations of counterfeit Christianity have stripped this heartfelt expression of its essence, turning it into nothing more than a pious ceremony. But not so when a present day genuine body of Christ joins together to eat in fellowship. They enjoy real food and real communion. And there is nothing that defines fellowship better than the coming together of common hearts.

As they eat, they do so remembering not only Christ and their responsibility before Him, but also their accountability toward each other. Since the poison of hypocrisy is simply not tolerated in their midst, they refuse to eat in fellowship with anyone they know is claiming Christianity while living unrepentant (I Corinthians 5:11). Please don't misunderstand. A true believer does not avoid worldly people as even Jesus ate with sinners (Matthew 9:10-11). It is the hypocrisy of pretense masked as authentic that threatens true fellowship among a genuine community. Therefore individuals examine themselves to avoid living unworthy before the Lord and among His body (I Corinthians 11:27-29). The concept of living a life set apart from this world is more than an ideal; it is a way of life.

The reality is that true community is an oasis, a refuge from the wickedness of the world and from the duplicity of the false church. Here there is no deceit, no insincerity, and no competition. Absent is the need to convince, the motive of selfishness, and the trappings of religion. Instead there is found an uncommon friendship where accountability is actually desired, not shunned. There exists within this community of believers a heart of surrendered brotherhood – unity of faith in the voice of God.

Psalms 107:35 expresses how God "changes a wilderness into a pool of water and a dry land into springs of water." He does this in a very real way in the midst of His church. But in order to see a spiritual desert changed into a thriving oasis requires that the members of the body actually *have* the life-altering water. In John 7:38, Jesus proclaimed that, "He who believes in Me, as the Scripture said, 'From his innermost being will flow rivers of living water.' " Thus in order to genuinely experience the water of life, believing – trusting in the voice of Christ – is an absolute essential. And since a church includes many believers (Romans 12:5), corporate accountability to continue in that faith becomes paramount.

Although we must all give an account to God on that day (Romans 14:12), it is those God has placed in leadership positions who must endure a far stricter accountability (James 3:1). The responsibility to oversee a true community of believers involves not only hearing and teaching the truth, but also identifying false doctrine, false believers, and wolves that would infiltrate an otherwise safe environment. These leaders test every spirit to see if it is from God (I John 4:1) in order to protect the flock under their care. And this is no easy task. Unlike counterfeit ministers who avoid confrontation for fear of losing their job, an authentic shepherd will run off the wolves that come for selfish gain, ego, or control. True overseers do not bow to political correctness, manmade rules, or a majority vote. They must answer to God – and God alone.

Since an authentic body has Christ as its head (Colossians 1:18), He alone determines position, direction, and structure. When

God desires to assemble several genuine believers together, *He* will choose a shepherd to oversee them and make His choice evident. The Lord will pick a *man* (I Timothy 2:12) who is not a recent convert (I Timothy 3:6), and will use him to train up the believers under his care (I Timothy 4:11, I Thessalonians 5:12). Also, as is seen throughout the New Testament, God often raises up a plurality of leadership within a church to help with the ministerial responsibilities. These leaders function to teach, rebuke, and aid in hearing the direction of the Lord.

Ephesians 4:12-16 gives a quick overview of what these leaders and their training will ultimately produce. Every follower is to be trained to completion, so that they are fully equipped for whatever work the Lord desires (12). Each believer is also taught to have unity in the faith, meaning that he hears the voice of God and trusts it to complete obedience as one with the entire fellowship (13). Thus the body is built up in the knowledge of Jesus until it reaches the "fullness of Christ" (13). This level of maturity is designed for much more than just doctrinal bragging rights or to attain the respect of men. A mature knowledge of Christ trains the fellowship to no longer be "tossed here and there by waves and carried about by every wind of doctrine, by the trickery of men, by craftiness in deceitful scheming" (14). Ultimately, the entire church will be able to speak the truth – the unveiled reality revealed by God – and to speak it in love (15).

This leadership of an uncommon community allows Christ to duplicate Himself in them – and they in turn duplicate themselves in each new Exception. Because the overseers of a genuine body do not hide secret hypocrisy, they are able to humbly urge the believers to "follow [their] example" (II Thessalonians 3:9). Upon the application of this whole-hearted life, each genuine Christian is then encouraged to become an example that others may follow (I Timothy 4:12, Titus 2:7).

True teachers within an authentic church convey so much more than a common creed, a page of concepts, or rules disguised as 'principles.' They do not teach selfish prosperity doctrines, dishonest positive confession, or a watered down salvation that has no real deliverance from sin. Instead, they teach heart. They teach how to see and walk out the truth as God reveals it. They teach how to die to self in order to know God and be in full agreement with Him. And once trained, a student of the spoken word of God will understand what it means to have corporate harmony in addition to individual peace.

Now, some might struggle with the concern that a leader who 'hears God' has no real accountability. This mindset generally comes from a belief that God doesn't *really* speak and therefore people who say God speaks to them are going to do whatever they want to. First, know for certain that any leader who *doesn't* hear God speak is a *false* teacher. But not so for a true man of God. The fact is that Jesus' sheep hear His voice (John 10:27) and He hasn't changed that (Hebrews 13:8). Secondly, if the body of believers is genuine, God will place true brothers within the church who are able to confirm what has been spoken. Otherwise the group is nothing more than a bunch of flakey, counterfeit Christians playing church.

This group accountability to the voice of God should not be mistaken for a power struggle that is implemented by public opinion or majority vote. God is real and continually makes His will known to the church. This gives the leadership not only multiple ears to hear, but multiple opportunities to hear as well. Therefore, decisions are never based on preference or appearance, but are based on a "righteous judgment" (John 7:24). Righteousness, once again, is to be right with God based on trust in His voice (Romans 4:9). And it is to this end that a genuine body of Christ will constantly redirect itself.

When these true believers come together there is not even the slightest hint of hype, propaganda, or self-promotion. The messages are taught in order to build up the body, and come from the voice of God, not from a dead denominational hand out or a watered down pastor's commentary. And since the Holy Spirit leads the instruction, there is no form of manipulation, no statements made for shock value, or demonstrative actions feigned for attention.

There is, however, passion. The leadership of an uncommon community has passion for God – and passion for His word.

They are diligent in "accurately handling the word of truth" (II Timothy 2:15) in order to feed the hungry sheep of their flock. The life of the fellowship actually depends on "every word that proceeds out of the mouth of God" (Matthew 4:4), both individually and collectively. It is therefore essential that God's will not only be taught, but also established within the hearts of the people.

The passion for the truth that is found in the leadership of the church is also revealed within the worship of a true body of Christ. When they come together to give glory to God in song, there is no hype, no showmanship, and no forced worship. Also absent from the meeting is an obligation to conform outwardly or to 'act' a certain way – as well as the half-hearted, superficial compliance to such a compulsion. Instead there is heartfelt contemplation, passionate enthusiasm, and a joyful anticipation of the presence of God within their midst. This type of worship is prayer, communion with God through song, and it is kept unadulterated from the flesh of religion. And those who lead such worship are in that position not based on their charisma or musical ability, but based on the fact that the voice of God has put them there. The overall goal is never to have exciting worship; it is to find God in the moment and give Him glory – the value that He is due.

This assembly is the true church of the Living God and not a 'McChurch' with self-centered 'express worship' and a twenty minute (or less) sermonette. And yet there is no glory given to long meetings either. When the people pray it is honest, it is deep, and it is from the heart rather than a written page. The leaders don't glory in their positions, fleece the sheep with 'Christian' moneymaking schemes, or allow Jezebels to grandstand and control. There is no wife swapping, gun stock piling, or pressure to move into the same subdivision. The clothes worn before the Lord on Sunday are the same clothes worn before Him at home on Saturday. And when all is said and done, God gets the praise and not man.

I find it intriguing that when religious people hear about a genuine body of Christ, they feel the need to vilify and categorize it. They will label it a fly-by-night sect, a cult, or a group of scoundrels with nefarious plans to con gullible people. They will label it anything *but* the true church. Why? Because the religious don't follow God wholeheartedly with passion at their church – thus anyone who does *must* be faking it. This is a very common perception. Since these religious, counterfeit believers secretly reject God while 'saying' that they are following Him, they are justified in their minds that everyone else must be too. All of this presumption takes place without them ever seeking God to know the truth. The few who do start to open their eyes either repent and find God, or in offense attack with slander and jealously. For the children of God, the fact will always remain that the world just doesn't know them (I John 3:1). But God does, and He considers them beautiful.

> *And the Lord their God will save them in that day*
> *as the flock of His people; for they are as the*
> *stones of a crown, sparkling in His land.*
> *Zechariah 9:16*

It is said that beauty is in the eye of the beholder. And yet we know that neither the world nor the religious find any loveliness in the authentic church. They do not because they choose not. How could the self-contaminated possibly be able to perceive the splendor of people who love God with all their hearts? They cannot for they are infected with love of self. God however, finds His bride beautiful and views her with significance, usefulness, and worth. He sees the hearts that hear, trust, and fully obey Him – and He sees them with so much value that they are compared to the sparkling jewels of a crown. *This* is the type of glory that God will place upon His royal brow. God knows these hearts, hearts that He has drawn to Himself and changed by the influencing of His grace – and He is *pleased*. God has set them apart by washing them with His voice (Ephesians 5:26) so that He may present them to Himself – spotless (27).

This uncommon community, these sold out believers live in such a way that they prove their innocence and blamelessness by living above reproach in this crooked and perverse generation (Philippians 2:15). Not only do they bring glory and value to their God, but they also shine as bright lights in this world (15). Regardless of the circumstance, the difficulty, or the suffering – the true body of Christ will hold fast to the spoken word of life (16) – and they will never let it go.

Application Summary

If you become part of the true church, you will find an uncommon community of believers different from everything that tries to pass itself off as the real thing. To be this type of worshiper you will have laid down your life – dying to yourself and all the flesh associated with it. You have chosen to respond to the grace influence of God and have been changed by Him, trusting in His voice to obedience. And as unique as you are following God wholeheartedly by yourself – imagine what it would be like to meet with others of like heart and mind.

As genuine followers of God, you do not meet together because of some common cause, a shared doctrinal stance, or a mutual income level. You won't care about the building, how cool the atmosphere is, or how slick the billboard advertising is. You meet together because God speaks and He said so. And you will practice hearing and trusting the voice of God as one – seeking God's will together. This practicing of righteousness not only keeps you in agreement with God, but each other as well. If there is a difference of opinion, God – who is real – will reveal who is and who is not following Him. Thus in the true church, you are able to distinguish between those who are really serving Him and those only going through the motions.

In this uncommon fellowship, it is a common practice for you to pray without ceasing. You will have a relationship with God that is in real time, open and completely honest with Him in every thought. In this way you will always have an ear to hear

His voice in every moment and be able to catch the revelation of His will. Though you may be mocked by the world and the religious alike, you will be standing on the solid bedrock established by God – a foundation that cannot be moved.

Hell will fear you. The gates of hell know that they cannot stand against a child who has the spoken word of God and who lives in that authority every moment. You are different. You are changed. You are not your own. The demons will now know your name and shudder because of the presence of God in you. You will burn bright and be as a light to other Exceptions who are willing to perceive.

And you will teach them, train them, and disciple them to the point that they not only hear the voice of God for themselves, they trust it to complete obedience. After they have surrendered all and God has confirmed it, they will trust His voice to be baptized – making the commitment to live and die for the cross. Then the demons will add their name to the list of believers that they fear.

When your uncommon community joins together to eat the Meal, you will not go through hollow formality and ritual ceremony, you will eat. You will sit and eat real food with real people who all follow a very real God. You will hold others accountable to live and eat without hypocrisy – and they will hold you accountable as well. In this you will find joy and peace, not discord and dishonesty. You are a surrendered brotherhood. You have found God's oasis in a desert of worldliness.

The leaders of this body are held to an even higher accountability before God and before one another. And this is the way it should be. As shepherds of God's flock, they willingly protect the sheep, not their paycheck. Your leadership will run off the wolves and the Jezebels, and stand aggressively against the influx of false doctrines. These are men of God. No manipulation, 'good idea,' or majority vote will influence the direction of the church – God is head, and He determines the right course.

In this body of Christ you will find a passion for truth – not political correctness. You will find a passion for God – not numerical validation. Worship is neither religiously hyped nor traditionally dead. And unlike so many counterfeit churches that squeeze God in on Sunday morning or glory in their lengthy services, you and your brethren meet as long as is necessary – and the glory goes to God.

As people who are God's possession, your fellowship is beautiful in His eyes. He washes you with the water of His voice removing the dirt and the dryness of this world. Are you perfect in every way? No – but you are honest, you are growing, and you are passionate for the Father. Yes, you may be demonized, hated, and persecuted by the jealous motives of the half-hearted, but it is a small thing compared to an eternity with Christ. And the light that He has given to you will shine so brightly that it will serve as a beacon to draw the next generation to the one and only truth.

<u>Challenging Your Perception</u>

1. Can you see how people who genuinely walk with God come together as a community of believers that is different from every other church that meets in pretense?

2. Do you perceive that the true church is more than just a dysfunctional family that sings pretty music, pools their opinions, and puts words in God's mouth to do as they please?

3. Are you willing to be changed by God in such a way as to become a pure bride for Christ? Will you be satisfied with less?

<u>Endnotes</u>

1. Spiros Zodhiates, TH.D., *The Complete Word Study Dictionary New Testament*, D/B/A AMG Publishers, copyright 1992 by Spiros Zodhiates and AMG International Inc., page 1154, Greek #4074, *petros*.

2. James Strong, LL.D., S.T.D., *The New Strong's Exhaustive Concordance of the Bible*, Dictionary of the Greek Testament, copyright 1990 by Thomas Nelson Publishers, page 57, Greek #4073, *petra*.

3. Spiros Zodhiates, TH.D., *The Complete Word Study Dictionary New Testament*, D/B/A AMG Publishers, copyright 1992 by Spiros Zodhiates and AMG International Inc., page 1154, Greek #4073, *petra*.

4. Ibid., page 1199, Greek #4198, *poreuomai*.

5. James Strong, LL.D., S.T.D., *The New Strong's Exhaustive Concordance of the Bible*, Dictionary of the Greek Testament, copyright 1990 by Thomas Nelson Publishers, page 59, Greek #4198, *poreuomai*.

6. Spiros Zodhiates, TH.D., *The Complete Word Study Dictionary New Testament*, D/B/A AMG Publishers, copyright 1992 by Spiros Zodhiates and AMG International Inc., page 936, Greek #3100, *matheteuo*.

7. Eberhard Arnold, *The Early Christians*, the Plough Publishing House of The Woodcrest Service Committee, Inc., paperback with permission by Baker Book house 1979, page 14.

8. Ibid., page 323.

9. Ibid., page 15.

10. Ibid., page 10.

How is it that churches are now worshipping in 'consecrated buildings,' with fixed forms of service, with rites, and numerous other ecclesiastical innovations? It is certain that none of this came from the New Testament.

Arthur Wallis

By what wicked courtesy of language is it, that the name of 'Christianity' has flattered this wretched system?

William Wilberforce

Let it be understood that those who are not living by Christ's teachings are not Christians at all – even though they might profess his teaching with their lips.

Justin Martyr

We should actually be meek, devout, and loving – not just simply seem to be.

Clement

Chapter

10

THE HARLOT CHURCH
(Religious Prostitution in the Name of God)

"See how the faithful city has become a harlot!"
Isaiah 1:21 NIV

The dawn after the feast, our hero awakens to a bustling society. He sees both men and women going about their daily responsibilities in the cool of the morning, while a group of children can be heard reciting the day's lesson in a nearby school room. An attentive young man is standing nearby to serve as the hero's guide for the day. No building is off limits, no question is too sensitive. After an hour or so of meandering, the hero sees a path leading out the back side of the village. Noticing the inquisitive look on the hero's face, the young tour guide motions for him to follow, and together they hike a short distance from the community.

As the hero crests a small hill, he sees to his surprise a small modern township complete with opened entry gates and a welcome sign. Upon walking in, he notices the pale streets are congested with throngs of – well, for lack of a better term – normal looking people. But who are they and how did they get out here in the Forbidden Zone? The guide explains that over the years many people had traveled to their village following the voice of the stones. But only a very few had the heart and integrity to put the stones in their rightful places upon the wall. Most however, coveted the power of the magical gems for themselves and after refusing to let go, ended up here in this settlement. They now scurry about, engrossed in self-absorbed thought and clinging to lifeless stones that have long since grown dull and silent.

"Come meet with us here at the Sapphire Building!" shrieks an old woman as she clutches the hero's arm. "No! No! Come to the meeting of the Amethysts! We are the real thing!" exclaims another pulling at his jacket. The hero quickly wrenches his arm away from the first frantic woman causing her to drop the elaborate case she is carrying in her other hand. The lid pops open and a faded blue stone falls unceremoniously into the mud. The scuttle begins to draw the attention of others who quickly clamor for the hero's attention. It is then that he and his guide decide to make a hasty exit toward the gate. As the duo leave the town and follow the trail back to the simplicity of the village, the echoes of those who possess garnet can be heard throwing insults at those possessing jade.

☙❧☙❧☙❧☙❧☙❧☙❧☙❧☙❧

As our hero learned, there are always people who claim to be genuine, and they are fully convinced in themselves that it is so. As long as they don't look deeper or question the possibility of error, they can continue to trust in their own understanding. If on the other hand they were to ask the hard questions and turn their ear to God, they would encounter a life-altering revelation. So let's ask those hard questions in relation to the church.

Why is the 'church' not what it should be? Why the disparity compared to the early church? Why is there rampant outward and hidden sin? Why are the 'Christians' of today's church saved only in concept but not actually delivered from their sin? Why the selfishness, materialism, and ego-centric lifestyle of its leadership? The brutal, cold dose of reality is: because it is not the church. Simply stated, the 'church' at large – that which generally purports itself to be the church – is not the true church.

If I call a mud puddle the ocean, it doesn't make it so; if I call Jell-O® icing, it doesn't change the fact that it is not; and just because unregenerate, religious individuals call themselves 'Christians' and call their meetings 'church,' it still remains that they are a group of undelivered people meeting under a false pretense. Their false labels serve as nothing more than a cloak of deception to psychologically warm their misperceptions.

And this really is quite common, having happened many times throughout history involving those who claimed to be God's people. Even today there are multitudes of denominations and cults alike egotistically claiming the title of doctrinal purity in contrast to the scriptural proofs that I have laid out for you in prior chapters. What is the result when generations of religious leaders continue to carry out plans that are not the Lord's (Jeremiah 18:12), when they do not ask "Where is the Lord?" (Jeremiah 2:8), and when they follow the presumption of their own perception rather than obeying the voice of God? The result is harlotry: religious prostitution in the name of God.

The Harlot Church has taken the possibility of a profound, intimate relationship with God and like a common whore perverted it, cheapening it for her own selfish gain. This lust for sordid gain – rather than God – turns intimacy into self-love, changes obedience into ritual and ceremony, and deforms a vital relationship of hearing and trusting God into a shallow compliance to the precepts of Scripture. Any revelation of God given to remedy the wickedness of her heart is quickly exchanged for a corrupted understanding in order to appear right in her own eyes. Sadly, even when confronted with such obvious truth, the harlot is brazen and refuses to blush with shame (Jeremiah 3:3).

And for what does this frequented prostitute sell herself for? What is so valuable to her that she ignores every attempt by

God to bring her to repentance? Men. She lusts to be intimate with men. The Harlot Church longs so greatly to gain the respect, approval, and love of men that she will rush like a donkey in heat to please her lovers (Jeremiah 2:24). To be right in the eyes of men is far more important to her than to be pure in the eyes of God. If you were to speak to her and say, "Where is the Lord?" or "Let's wait for God to speak and then in agreement together obey Him no matter the cost" – the Harlot Church will ignore your voice just as she does the voice of God. The response will be one of offense, self-importance, and theological vomit. Then, true to form, she will brazenly continue down her own path to do as she pleases, lusting after the opinions of men. I tell you the truth – the whore will have her reward. And I am sad to say that we are a nation of whores.

In order to achieve the depraved goal of pleasing men, the harlot has plastered herself with the make-up of this world, has dressed herself seductively, and has placed her confidence in her tainted outward attractiveness. Her flesh boisterously proclaims upon the slick billboard advertising – "I am the church with money; I am the church with status; I am the church that pretty people attend." And if you go to her self-glorified buildings to witness her self-serving meetings – and if you have eyes to see – you will also discover the telling truth that in her self-determined actions, she is also proclaiming, "I am my own god."

God's message to the false church of this generation can be quoted directly out of Ezekiel 16:15-16:

> *But you trusted in your beauty and played the harlot because of your fame, and you poured out your harlotries on every passer-by who might be willing. You took some of your clothes, made for yourself high places of various colors and played the harlot on them, which should never come about nor happen.*

You should know, therefore, that the competition for the admiration of man is fierce. "We are the largest, we are the best, we are the most spiritual! Come and visit us where you are loved and desired and lusted after!" Good facilities will attract the self-absorbed and the fleshly. The naïve are deceived and accepted because of a quick, non-delivering prayer. And then the value of their number and the value of their tithe are garnered by the whore to justify a ministry based on false doctrine and the arm of man.

The prostitute would say, "I have spread my couch with coverings, with colored linens of Egypt. I have sprinkled my bed with myrrh, aloes and cinnamon" (Proverbs 7:16-17). A convincing ruse, yet the trappings of the bondage of Egypt will never deliver you from the chains of slavery – no matter how nice the smell. Even the good things of God – those things that actually bring about deliverance and relationship – when found in the hands of the religious, are twisted into something more self-serving, or misshaped into something far less convicting. Ezekiel 16:17 says:

> *You also took your beautiful jewels made of My*
> *gold and of My silver, which I had given you, and*
> *made for yourself male images that you might*
> *play the harlot with them.*

As unattractive as this might seem to us, imagine how ugly this is when God sees how the Harlot Church mistreats the valuable things He has given – like truth, salvation, and Scripture – in order to appear beautiful *to men*.

But this painted lady doesn't concern herself with the heart of God, for she has "played the harlot after the gods of the peoples of the land" (I Chronicles 5:25). She sets up these idols right in the middle of the church because they make her all the more attractive to her lovers. She propagates positions, titles, degrees, paychecks, clothing, and reputation. All of which do nothing for the kingdom of God, but everything for the kingdom of man. If she doesn't follow the same idols as the men she loves, she knows they will soon ostracize her, cast her out, and reject her for another who will tickle their itching ears (II Timothy 4:3). And that just won't do.

Instead, the harlot is boisterous in the streets, lurking on every corner (Proverbs 7:11-12). "We are trying to reach men for Jesus," is the claim. And without following the voice of God, or even the Scripture for that matter, the streetwalker goes from door to door to find her next encounter. She brazenly uses the wickedness of the world to advertise her wares. Materialism, bribery, and slick slogans are all used to attract the gullible. Then man-made formulas and the comfort of false doctrines are engaged to keep them. Oh, I agree that she *is* trying to reach men, just not for Jesus. She works her seduction to fully ensnare those who lack sense (Proverbs 7:7), and then is quick to tack God's name on her efforts.

Many will flock to such local, religious whorehouses to get their spiritual fix on Sunday. They gladly surrender true intimacy with God in order to get the satisfaction of a psychological 'feel good.' And then the transaction occurs: I'll accept you if you accept me; I'll ignore your sin if you ignore mine; I'll make you feel good if you make me feel good. God is then given mere lip service as the harlot and her lover engage in an ungodly alliance of self-interest (Isaiah 30:1).

Such spiritual harlotry may have an *appearance* of righteousness (Ezekiel 16:51-52). But this façade is nothing more than the means by which the Harlot Church conceals her shamefulness and attracts the people who will give her the attention she craves. Seductively, she bats her eyes and musters all the false humility she can as she deceptively confesses to the world that she follows God and calls Him Father and friend. Yes, this is how she talks, but then she selfishly does all the evil she can (Jeremiah 3:4-5).

As previously discussed in chapter one, to actually perceive the ancient path of God it becomes important to stand and see the other roads before you. Since the false church is one of the more popular broad roads and is followed by so many, the need to stand and take an honest look at its practices is paramount.

This leads us to the main verse for this chapter, Isaiah 1:21(NIV):

See how the faithful city has become a harlot!

Will you see how the faithful ministry, which once trusted in the voice of God, has become a painted whore that seeks value from the hand of man? Will you choose to gaze past the deceptive wizard's curtain and see how that which is purported as genuine is actually nothing more than a well executed scam? Will you see that it is the *True* Church, not the Harlot Church, which is God's chosen institution and avenue for change? In dealing with the Harlot Church, Ezekiel 16:37 states that God will "expose [her] nakedness to them that they may see all [her] nakedness." Thus, to help you in your endeavor I would like to share with you several specifics easily observed relating to these religious social clubs. If you are the Exception, let these embolden your spirit – let them add to the fire caused by the injustices that you have seen . . .

Have you been accosted by religious junk mail begging for money? If you will send in a seed offering they will sell you – I mean send you – a prayer rug. Just kneel on the anointed rug and receive what you ask for. Or pray this prayer of Saint So-and-so to be blessed in more ways then you can imagine. Do you wish to be healed? *You can be* by using this vial of holy 'insert the desired liquid here.' You can even put this special spiritual whatchamacallit under your pillow to grow hair or put it under your checkbook to be financially blessed. Sister So-and-so did it just last month and received five thousand dollars in the mail. Just send in your love offering AND ALL THIS CAN BE YOURS! (Yes they even use all caps.)

Maybe you have received the 'We're the coolest youth group in town' flyer. It comes with full-color pictures of the youth facility and explanation of the latest video game system give away. Door prizes and loud music – even a slightly used car will be drawn for. When the local newspaper asks the youth minister about the questionable tactics he says, "Well if the world uses those tactics, why can't we?" Yeah, what's a little more plastered make-up to a whore?

Have you seen the 'Christian' T.V. commercials that target the weak by saying, "Never be a victim again – just send in this love offering to get help." So much for not being a victim again. Or maybe you have seen the poor, starving children of Africa shamelessly used by religious men. The children are told to walk slowly by the camera and frown, and then after the hard sell guilt trip, they are told to smile and act happy. Look, poor children! What are you, heartless? Do you *want* them to die? Never once does the commercial act Christian by mentioning to wait on God, to hear His voice, or to seek His will. And yet, the most wicked sales pitch I have seen was at a 'Christian' concert that said you were not really saved if you didn't give to their cause – after all, if you really were a Christian you'd give. This supposed 'ministry' doesn't care if you *want* to be influenced by *God* just as long as you *are* influenced by *them*.

As you drive down the street you may see a vast array of billboards advertising the best churches in town. High dollar ad agencies with slick slogans hype the value of the local religious brothels. Do you want to be accepted, loved, and cared for like no other? We have many ministers to tend to your wants – I mean needs. Come to our 'pretty people' church where no one would dare question your validity. If you say you are okay, that's fine with us. We just want you to come and give us value! (Those seeking genuine salvation need not apply.)

When you drive into the church parking lot, pay close attention. You will find the pastor's name arrogantly displayed on the sign out front. It is there for *you* to see, so make sure you don't miss it. Also the congregation is very proud of its facility, so much so that the church building is prominently displayed on all the business cards and stationery. The unspoken truth among the more wealthy members is that the value of the ministry is proportionate to the amount of money spent on the church building. I mean, come on! Success in the ministry is the same as success in the world, right? Even the accomplishment of a preacher's ministry is tied to both the numeric growth and new construction of the church. If membership numbers are increased or a new building is raised, so the perceived value of the minister is enhanced. But should that same preacher take an honest stand against the false doctrine of the church, call out the sin of the congregants, or require the leadership to *actually* hear, trust, and obey God – he will be shown the door.

Generally, you will find that the financial bracket of the congregation you visit will determine the warmth of a church. The poorer the church is – the more friendly and needy; the wealthier the church is – the more cold and distant. Regardless of status, they both lack true relationship with God and thus have to fake true community. Sure you may find cliques that have an appearance of spiritual relationship – *just don't speak the truth*. If you do, it will get ugly and ugly quick. Most in the service will nod and play their part while proclaiming that they are different when they really are not. Sure, they are religious – and thus different to a degree – but their doctrine of repentance is so askew that they have become quite comfortable living in the deception of false salvation. Imagine sitting down in the false church and asking the person next to you, "What did God speak to you today?" You will receive a 'don't speak to me you freak' stare or an uncontrolled blather describing the demon claws seen in the spirit realm that scratched down the walls of the sanctuary.

Worship . . . is a gamble. Value may be placed on the pipe organ's beautiful sound, or the value may very well be on the fact that there is an absence of an organ. The music can be anything from liturgical, classical, and heartless – to up-tempo, contemporary, and contrived. So much of traditional worship has a simulated, fabricated sense of life – while contemporary worship is quite often a conjured, forced, and strained divination to get God to 'move.' Despite the style, worship leaders are often guilty of 'stirring the Spirit if the Spirit isn't stirring.' Well, the Spirit left a long time ago – but ya'll go on ahead without Him.

Of course the local preacher/politician/game show hosts have to get their paychecks, so right before the offering prayer I once heard it stated (and I kid you not) – "Did you know that God can't do anything without money?" And it was answered by a thousand hearty amens. Then the prayer ensues . . . "Lord I give you this offering knowing you will protect me from evil . . ." as if God was some kind of street corner shake down thug offering 'protection' for pay. Make sure you give your money to God (through this local branch office) or else the Devil's gonna getcha! Besides – giving these indulgences to God is like having your very own personal Santa machine. Thank ya Jesus.

If you visit on a fifth Sunday you may get to experience communion. No, it won't be a heartfelt meal of fellowship like that found in the Bible or like the early Christians experienced. Instead it will be nothing more than a pious ritual of eating a small, dry piece of cracker and drinking an almost non-existent thimble of grape juice. No accountability, no fellowship, and no indication that anyone cares enough to change it. That is with the exception of those with the new 'Rock Concert Communion' concept. This is a new – bad – idea from the flesh of wicked ministers in an attempt to pump life back into what has become a dead and lifeless ceremony. I mean come on, how else are we going to get college students to look toward the church unless we dress her up like the world and pimp her out like a common whore? Apparently repentance is out of the picture, huh?

The preacher of a Harlot Church is given the job not based on the voice of God, a delivered life, or the fact that he loves God with all his heart. No, he is chosen as a CEO is chosen to run a corporation. He needs experience, success in past churches numerically and financially – and he needs a piece of paper from a school saying that other spiritually dead intellectuals approve of his false doctrine. There is a tendency, however, for small churches to hire new young Bible students. This is often done by deacon boards who like to keep a firm grasp on control. Just as long as the man of God isn't too much of a 'man' things will go swimmingly. The final hiring decision, though, as is true with the world, comes down to money. The Harlot Church is cheap, but not usually that cheap when it comes to salaries. It's gonna cost you. After all, it costs a lot of money to get that framed piece of paper to hang on the wall behind the desk – right there for everyone to see.

Next, we come to the token prayer. It may be long or short, monotone or impassioned, written down beforehand or momentarily inspired. But token nonetheless. It is not prayed because someone follows the leadership of the Spirit but because this is the place where the prayer goes – it says so right there in the bulletin. Of course an off the cuff 'I feel led' prayer may be voiced as long as it has the proper amount of warmth, emotion, and sincerity. Yet if you are at the Harlot Church – it is nothing more than a symbolic gesture that has become the new, expected, spontaneous tradition. The goal is never to be in actual agreement with God, but to keep the flesh unity of the assembly. Pray harder, pray longer, pray louder – just don't pray honestly. Tears, screams, and even pious posturing will always be preferred over true repentance and genuine brokenness. Of course they pray – the rule says they are supposed to.

When it comes to some of the messages, the preachers must be entertaining although they would never actually say so. Instead they use terms like inspiring, energetic, or exciting. But if you visit the more liturgical churches, don't worry, the lecture will be intellectually droned with the proper amount of pomp. Strangely, the more religious garb that is required for the speaker to wear – the more sanctimonious the message. Regardless of the type, know that these sermons have been painstakingly poured over because the security of the preacher's job can hang upon even one miscue. Performance is paramount since jobs, money, and the love of men are on the line. The best wolves know how to smoothly preach peace, peace, while thoroughly watering down true salvation. These snake oil salesmen don't study to show themselves approved; they study to convince, to justify, and to avoid costly embarrassment. The spoken word of truth won't be divided correctly, it'll be butchered. Rest assured that they will follow the demigod of unity, tolerance, and appeasement in order to preach a 'lowest common denominator gospel' at the cost of the cross. If the word 'Jesus' can at least demonically cross your lips – congratulations – you're in agreement with them!

The entire service in most churches comes down to the altar call. Don't take this lightly; the very value of the Harlot Church depends upon the approval of man. The whore needs something to happen or else she may start to question the validity of her ministry. Get them down the aisle! Have counselors come down at the same time to give the illusion that God is moving. Forget the fact that new followers are supposed to be discipled first and taught to surrender *all* their hearts in complete trust. Manipulate those white knuckle hold outs; they are about to crack! Then, if one or two finally get up enough nerve, they half-heartedly walk down to pray an unscriptural prayer 'work' because they fear hell or just want to be okay in their own eyes. Sadly, no one in the Harlot Church understands repentance or discipleship and is able to actually lead them to deliverance. Instead, the pastor will convince them that they have done enough, convince them they have given their lives, and convince them they are now secure no matter what. *Just make sure they believe what the false preacher says* – after all, isn't that faith? Get them to fill out the card and dunk them. Quick! It might not take! Tally that new high score and send it to the big boys upstairs. They need to know the numbers . . . because . . . well . . . they need to know. What if they don't have enough chairs, parking spaces, or classrooms . . . also people need to be encouraged by the growth of their church. It's just a small lie, just enough to give everyone deniability. But God sees all.

If no one is deceived enough to come down to the front and accept the wicked way – disguised as following Jesus – they will do something to make up for it. Invite the church members down to pray maybe. Still not enough? Okay, get them to come down and the pastor will pray for them. Pray for headaches, pray for finances, pray for marriages. Or get people to testify – anything to keep the illusion that God is moving among them. God forbid the truth come out that no one's heart was changed. They still believe the lie, they still have no real deliverance from their flesh, and they still hate the light that shines on them revealing the truth of their hearts. But hey, the headaches are gone, right?

The various mid-week Bible studies and prayer meetings are a hodge-podge of erroneous misperceptions. This is when the most zealous meet to pool their ignorance. And what a spectacle it is as the blind lead the blind in denominational pageantry. Their pride in the church's spiritual heritage is clung to as if the very fabric of all spiritual life depended on it. Religious men of old are elevated to 'pillar' status even though their doctrine is so poor that anyone with a concordance could prove them wrong. Apply a little heroification and these fallen individuals are turned into infallible, pious saints. Disagree with them and you will be mercilessly mocked and laughed at. For over 2,000 years, the religious have glorified the traditions of men that have muddied the spiritual waters of Christendom. It is as if Jesus never said traditions invalidate the commands of God. But then again, the Harlot Church isn't big on listening to the voice of God anyway.

Speaking of refusing to listen to the voice of God, we arrive at the church board meeting. One time, when a board was confronted with the need to wait on God to speak in order to know His will, I heard the response – and I quote, "If we waited for God to speak we wouldn't get anything done." I'm sorry, I didn't realize that the arm of man, doing what the mind of man determines is right was more important than the will of the Living God – my mistake. Then they sit around a table and help convince each other that they really do have faith until they reach the point that they feel good about the wicked state of their hearts.

Next, this gathering of deceived men – who refuse to hear God mind you – pray a hypocritical token prayer to be 'led' by the Spirit as *they* do what pleases *them*. And so the god of good ideas rears its ugly head again and the dumbed down ministry of man creates a cause – any cause – just to validate itself. Since they lack relationship with God, they settle with doing things as the world does them. No accountability to God, no accountability to the truth, and no accountability to anyone trying to show them the error of their ways.

Should any pastor rise up and try to actually *be* a shepherd, he will be so bullied that he will bend for the sake of compromise, unity, or his paycheck. The reality is that these preachers have to answer to the board that hires and fires if even the clothes they wear on Sunday morning don't meet expectations. So, most ministers remain so ingrained in the system that they will play their role as hired hands and do as they are told. If the Harlot Church were to lose a pastor over these issues, it's okay – there are plenty of other 'ministers' out there who want a paycheck and will be willing to tickle their itching ears.

These are just a few of the ways the harlot prostitutes herself for selfish gain. The scariest part of all this is that I didn't make any of it up – these are all true life examples. Now you may struggle with my bluntness and may even consider the fact that I spoke the honest truth mean spirited. I just think it is time to call a pig a pig. And I refuse to dance around the 800 pound gorilla in the room just because men don't want to acknowledge the obvious truth. II Timothy 4:3-4 says:

> *For the time will come when they will not endure*
> *sound doctrine; but wanting to have their ears*
> *tickled, they will accumulate for themselves*
> *teachers in accordance to their own desires, and*
> *will turn away their ears from the truth and will*
> *turn aside to myths.*

And I believe that time has come.

The Harlot Church is the problem, not the solution. A tawdry intimacy with man to feel good about your spiritual state does not translate into an intimate salvation with God. The attempt to gain recognition and popularity before man has not resulted in the deliverance of mankind but only in obtaining disgrace and infamy before the eyes of Him to whom we must give account. James 4:4 painfully asks the question, "You adulteresses, do you not know that friendship with the world is hostility toward God?" Yet so many people choose to straddle the fence when it comes to complete commitment to God. Sadly, the Harlot Church has no real answer to the rampant hostility it constantly displays before Him.

What solution does the harlot have for the person bound by sin other than a religious version of the world's best twelve-step program? The hard reality is that when a person needs deliverance, the false church "[promises] them freedom while they themselves are slaves of corruption" (II Peter 2:19). These charlatans ought to hold to the truth that "men should seek instruction from His mouth" (Malachi 2:7), but instead they have set aside what God has spoken "for the sake of their traditions" (Mark 7:13).

God, however, has not left these wolves in sheep's clothing alone. He has spoken to them in a variety of ways, though they may not perceive it (Job 33:14 NIV). Through the Scriptures, dreams, visions, words, nature, and even through men – God has let His voice be heard. Though He has tried to influence them, God says through Jeremiah, "they have turned their back to me and not their faces; though I taught them, teaching again and again, they would not listen and receive instruction" (Jeremiah 32:33).

To make the point even further, listen to what Isaiah said about the wicked church:

> *For this is a rebellious people, false sons, sons*
> *who refuse to listen to the instruction of the Lord;*
> *who say to the seers, "You must not see visions";*
> *and to the prophets, "You must not prophesy to us*
> *what is right, speak to us pleasant words,*
> *prophesy illusions. Get out of the way, turn aside*
> *from the path, let us hear no more about the Holy*
> *One of Israel."*
> *Isaiah 30:9-11*

Rebellious, false sons are the ones who refuse to listen to the Lord. False sons want to ignore the truth and be told pleasant illusions so they can continue in their own perceptions. These religious rebels don't want to walk the ancient path that has been laid out before them. Instead, they clamor like demons for permission to turn from that path – and yet they still claim the name of Christ.

"Our church is different." If I've heard it once, I've heard it a thousand times. Then a quick inspection into the veracity of the statement most often reveals two things: the fact that it is not different, and the reality that the person speaking is blind. "It must be where you live" is just another shallow attempt at avoiding the all too awful truth. "Well my preacher isn't that way." Is this the same preacher who doesn't believe God really speaks? Or says that God does speak, but then turns around and does as he pleases under the guise of obedience? Who rejects full surrender needed for salvation? Who leads people to 'salvation' in an unscriptural work of the sinner's prayer? Whose salvation doctrine has no real deliverance? Who baptizes the undiscipled? Who uses love and unity as excuses to not hold anyone accountable for their 'decision'? Who uses the Bible as a rule book claiming it is their final authority? Who defines grace as mercy? Whose faith is a mental acknowledgement? Whose forgiveness is only pardon? Who would strain out a 'gnat' when it comes to this very paragraph and yet swallow the 'camel' of their own wicked doctrine? *That* preacher?!

Don't make falsehood your refuge or conceal yourself with deception (Isaiah 28:15). Wake up and smell the burning sulfur. I encourage you to "see how the faithful city has become a harlot" (Isaiah 1:21NIV). Christendom does not need another revival, renewal, or reformation – what it needs is repentance. Look past the whitewash, the nice buildings, and the designer suites. Look past the smiles, persuasive words, and soft confident tones in the voice. Find the truth; find God. There is a reason people don't see the truth about the church today – simply put, they just don't want it to be true. And the real reason that people choose not to acknowledge this reality is self-preservation. If their church is not really 'The Church,' then they may not really be a Christian. Not being a genuine Christian means they will go to hell . . . and now we see the real motive.

The Harlot Church has taken the things of God – such as the Bible, the name 'Church,' and the term 'Christian' – and has "transformed the beauty of His ornaments into pride" (Ezekiel 7:20). This woman is no spotless bride. She is dry and dirty and far too common. With her hair a tangled mess, she yells like the brazen hussy to shut up – stop confronting her with the Holy One of Israel and just give her another drink so she can dull the voice of God in her head. Ugly game playing, ugly pretense, ugly distortion of the truth. Quick, slap some more lipstick on the pig, here comes another generation of the gullible. Sure, it works on those who have no sense, on those who will not see. But to the Exception, all the plastered makeup in the world won't hide the fact that she is nothing more than a cheap whore looking for her next fix. Pity her, but don't fall for her.

Application Summary

One of the harder questions you may ask yourself is – why isn't the church today like the church in the New Testament? Most will overlook the conundrum because it means little to them. But to those who will see the rampant undelivered selfishness, the fleshly outbursts, and the hidden sin – the painful truth is apparent. It is a meager fabrication; a mockery of the bride of Christ. The *True* Church, however, is *God's chosen institution* in this world. The false church lays claim to the title, but using the name 'Church' or 'Christian' does not make it so.

The false church has taken intimacy with God and exchanged it for intimacy with man for selfish gain. This religious prostitution of loving men and catering to men has turned what should be a spotless bride for God into a common spiritual harlot. She loves the feeling she gets when she pleases men. She even values the same idols that men love. Right in the middle of her services she shamelessly worships reputation, materialism, position, and false doctrine. In her pride she dresses like the world using any worldly way to further her attractiveness to her lovers. She trusts in her beauty and popularity. Confront her and she will ignore your voice just as she does God's. Even the spiritual things given by God like Scripture, truth, and salvation – she has twisted in order to please her own selfish desires.

Boisterous in the streets, the Harlot Church calls out brazenly through mail outs, billboard advertisements, and TV specials in order to seduce men with her attractiveness. She draws them in so she may play the harlot with them. If she gives them a psychological feel good, they in turn will validate her and give her the value she craves. Yes, she has an appearance of righteousness – but this is only a pretense. This seductress will wear whatever face is necessary to persuade the gullible. A deceptive smile on a well painted face – her beauty is only a façade.

But will you see it? Do you have the heart to look past the outer appearance and into the heart of such a beast? Ask God to help you perceive the difference between the true church and the one who plays the harlot. The time has come when the religious will gather to themselves teachers who will tell them what they want to hear. Sure, a little truth is sprinkled in to help keep up the illusion, but even the worldly can see the hypocrisy. Can you?

Friendship with the world is hatred toward God no matter how you twist it. And the Harlot Church loves the things of this world, especially the opinions and plans of men. Although the very Scripture they teach on Sundays clearly states that men should seek instruction from the mouth of God, they reject His voice and reject His truth. God has taught them again and again, but they would not listen. They are false sons walking a false path, following a false gospel. The Harlot Church is no spotless bride. She is not pure, clean, or honest. Don't fall for her deception. See past the game, past the lie. Don't make falsehood your refuge. Be different. Be the Exception.

Challenging Your Perception

1. Are you able to accept the fact that what is generally called 'the Church' is not the Church? Can you see how the Harlot Church

dresses herself up to please the lusts of men?

2. Do you find yourself shying away from this truth because you want to avoid rejection and the disapproval of men? Do you find that *you* have played the Harlot?

3. Are you willing to suffer at the hands of the Harlot for refusing her advances? Will you walk away from her even as she brazenly hurls insults at you?

The Pharisee is much more common than you think. Many 'Christians' try to lead 'good Christian lives' and are proud of themselves for it.

Fenelon

Are you living a lie?

Scott Gusa

They think that they can look upon their lives with an impartial eye and congratulate themselves on their inoffensiveness in society.

William Wilberforce

What is a faithless heart doing in a home of faith? Why is a person who does not completely trust in Christ even called a Christian? The name Pharisee is more fitting for such a one.

Cyprian

Chapter

11

FOLLOWER OR PHARISEE

(An Honest Look in the Mirror)

"How long will you hesitate between two opinions?"
1 Kings 18:21

As our hero returns from his excursion to the neighboring township, a slight, peculiar thought starts to whisper in his mind. It is clearly not the deep, profound type of voice that he had heard when listening to the stone; it is something far more insignificant, trivial even. But as it grows, the hero recognizes his own inner voice of compromise for what it is. He finds himself comparing the simplicity of the village to the modern amenities of the township. The notion of paved streets, nice buildings, and the comfort of air conditioning begins to tug at his reasoning. Does he *have* to live in the straw huts of the village? Can't he still explore the mysteries of the Forbidden Zone while living more comfortably in the township? Maybe he can have both. Maybe he can take just a small stone, one that wouldn't be missed. Imagine the power, what it could accomplish back at the township. He could change things, even bring the two settlements together.

Although the hero thinks he is alone with his thoughts, the villagers know the battle that he is engaged in. They recognize the situation – having seen it many times before with those who left for the luxury of pretense. Eventually, the newcomer will become so caught up in himself that no one will be able to convince him otherwise. But they know the hero must choose for himself. Would he choose comfort and compromise with the majority, or simplicity and genuineness with the few?

As the hero continues to contemplate his new dilemma, he finds himself standing in front of the sentient rock wall. He turns to notice that the villagers are beginning to bring out food for another feast. A new traveler is on the way. The children begin to giggle as the air fills with the wondrous smell of food. It is then that the hero knows he has made his decision.

ശ൯ൠൟൠൟശ൯ൠൟൠൟശ൯ൠൟൠൟശ൯ൠൟൠൟശ൯ൠൟൠ

Choice. You have a God-given free will to choose to follow God or reject Him. You also have the free will to start following God and then to turn away from Him if you so choose. And, regardless of what the modern-day Gnostics would tell you, it is ultimately your decision to determine how you will live out your spiritual life. Therefore, in the process of choosing whether or not to walk down God's ancient path, you will have to decide if you want to become a follower or a Pharisee.

Biblically, the Pharisees were a religious and political group that was constantly antagonistic toward Jesus and His followers. Although they claimed to serve the Living God, they did all in their power to resist Him. Under the cloak of religion, they badgered Jesus as He taught, spread outright lies about Him among the people, and were even successful in plotting His death. This group of pious preachers was so wicked in their self-serving, religious behavior that today the term Pharisee has come to define the very essence of self-righteousness.

The truth is that many 'Christians' are modern-day Pharisees; false followers who are non-Christian Christians. Their doctrinal sheep's clothing has become so convincing to the world that they are considered the quintessential believer. As they go through the motions of religion, they claim they are 'following Jesus'; as they remain in the bondage to self-desire, they assert that they are 'delivered'; and as they spew out the poison of a false salvation to the masses, they proclaim that they are 'evangelizing.'

Millions of Pharisees are fully convinced in themselves that their recipe for salvation is complete. Start with a large bowl (a narrow one just won't do), add in a generous amount of God's mercy (avoiding the sticky mess of God's changing grace), then a couple of sincere emotions (sorrow and joy look spiritual, don't they?), and last but not least, add in a dash of works (like praying the sinner's prayer). Bake it all in the passionate fire of self-determination – and what do you have? You have a half-baked, half-hearted excuse for a true follower of God.

These self-serving, self-convinced pseudo-believers are bold to engage in countless causes, church functions, and spiritual discussions – all apart from God – and then hypocritically tack God's name on it. Although they try to gloss over their dead works with good intentions, it does not change the inherent ugliness. Many pharisaical 'believers' will stand before God on that day and be fully convinced that *in His name* they prophesied, cast out demons, and even performed miracles. Then Jesus will say to them, "I never knew you, depart from me you who practice lawlessness" (Matthew 7:22-23). Though this is the hard reality, to try to convince them otherwise is a monumental feat that quite often ends in futility.

You might be saying, "But all these so-called Pharisees seem so zealous for God." Paul testified about them in his day and indicated that they did indeed have such fervor:

For I testify about them that they have a zeal for
God, but not in accordance with knowledge. For
not knowing about God's righteousness and
seeking to establish their own,

they did not subject themselves to the
righteousness of God.
Romans 10:2-3

Zeal without the true knowledge of God only propagates deeds that originate from the flesh. Of what value is the zealous religious labor of man? Sadly, to the local church, it is the stuff that keeps the cogs turning. But as Paul said in the verse above, this type of enthusiasm and commitment – that is labeled 'for God' – is in no way righteous. It is self-initiated and self-sustained. And we know that if God did not initiate it, if His voice is not trusted, and if the action is not carried out to the point of complete obedience – it will never be accepted as right in the sight of God.

But failure to be right with God never stops the selfishness of religious men from seeking out what pleases their flesh. They will search high and low for a belief system that will justify their own understanding. All this effort is expended just to be right in their own eyes. But do the pious pretenders have the same zeal to search out God to find *His* will? Does their dedication compel them to search the Scripture to find the truth, the way to be right with God? No. Neither do they have ears to hear when someone clearly spells out the truth for them. Even if the best and brightest of Pharisees does go that extra mile to actually find some small scrap of truth, it will be quickly misshapen to conform to the dogma of men. Even the meaning of this very paragraph will be twisted and contorted in order to justify the flesh when it is read by a Pharisee.

This brings us to one of the core realities involving the pharisaical lifestyle – hypocrisy. The religious hypocrite lives a lifestyle of pretense, falsely claiming to serve God while actually serving the self. This spiritual double standard has every appearance of piety, with its seemingly biblical basis and spiritual preoccupation – but this devotional duplicity never actually surrenders self-interest or engages God.

Jesus Himself made this point when he saw firsthand the Pharisees' outward charade. In Matthew 23:25, He declared,

"Woe to you, Scribes and Pharisees, hypocrites! For you clean the outside of the cup and the dish, but inside they are full of robbery and self-indulgence." Of what value is it before God to follow religious rules and principles outwardly only to leave the inward sin of self intact? "You blind Pharisee, first clean the inside of the cup and dish, so that the outside of it may become clean" (26).

True righteousness comes from trusting and obeying what God speaks to you. As you follow His guidance, every aspect of your heart will be changed by the hand of God. This is far more substantial than just whitewashing your public image before men so you will "appear beautiful" in their eyes (27). If, in your religious efforts, your heart remains selfish – "So you, too, outwardly appear righteous to men, but inwardly you are full of hypocrisy and lawlessness" (28).

As it is easier to cut off a piece of fruit from a tree than it is to kill the fruit tree at its root – so it is far easier to cease the outward aspects of sin than it is to die to the root desires that battle within the heart. When confronted with this dilemma, the Pharisee chooses the easy way out. But to constantly be dealing with the outward manifestation of the flesh is in no way repenting of the inward sin that is giving birth to that flesh in the first place. Even those who obey the voice of God may get caught up in this deception by only obeying outwardly. To drive the point home, let me remind you of King Amaziah, who after obeying outwardly, the Scriptures say that, "He did right in the sight of the Lord, yet not with a whole heart" (II Chronicles 25:2).

Does God speak to men for them to only follow Him in outward pretense? Or does God require us to love Him with ALL our heart, soul, mind, and strength? Are we to be delivered only from the sounds of the chains that bind us, or from the very chains themselves? Make no mistake; the pharisaical flesh that parades itself around as theological understanding will try to convince you, even now, that being completely delivered to follow God wholeheartedly is not required.

It is for this very reason that Jesus warns us to "Beware of the leaven of the Pharisees, which is hypocrisy" (Luke 12:1). Just like in a loaf of bread, the yeast of hypocritical half-heartedness will spread throughout not only an individual's heart – but the entire community of believers as well. "Do you not know that a little leaven leavens the whole lump of dough?" (I Corinthians 5:6). And in the case of this generation – I'm afraid it has.

Hypocrisy is at the very crux of what is falsely called contemporary Christendom. Millions upon millions of people profess to have 'given Jesus all their lives' only to live daily for themselves. Although they may even believe themselves to be sincere in their vow, the Scripture makes it clear that "It is better not to make a vow than to make a vow and not fulfill it" (Ecclesiastes 5:5 NIV). This reality is true to the point that "Cursed is the cheat" who vows to give God what is acceptable but then offers a "blemished" sacrifice (Malachi 1:14 NIV). As Hosea bluntly points out, "They speak mere words; with worthless oaths they make covenants" (Hosea 10:4). Let me stress this once again. According to Scripture – it is *better* to not even make a vow and say you 'give your life to Jesus' if in the process you never die to yourself and release control.

A Pharisee's seemingly sincere vow to live for God is not the organic relationship that God desires. For a Pharisee substitutes the reality of a genuine relationship with the Father for a legalistic observance of principles and rules. This legalism does not encumber itself with the heartfelt passion of seeking, hearing, and following the Spirit of the Living God. Instead, legalism makes adhering to what is written in the Scripture its main objective. Make no mistake; this action is hollow and meaningless before God, though the Pharisee may feel very pious and even emotional in the endeavor. The Apostle Paul pointed out, however, that we are to be servants "not of the letter but of the Spirit; for the letter kills" (II Corinthians 3:6). When a person is deceived to think that going through the *motions* of following God – *is following God*, those actions kill the very possibility of the relationship they were intended to create.

Lest you get confused, I am not saying that the Bible is not the written word of God, profitable for teaching, reproof, correction, and training in righteousness (II Timothy 3:16). Not at all. But what I am saying is that those principles *must* have life breathed into them by God to have any value. It is God's spoken word that is "living and active," and since we are not to interpret the Scriptures for ourselves (II Peter 1:20) – we need the Spirit of God to bring the letter to life. Without divine help, your self-perception of the Scripture will become nothing but a pharisaical presumption of its meaning.

This false practice of legalism is not limited to just a personal, religious belief exercised privately by the Pharisee. There are multiple rules that flow out of them and take many forms of deceptive teaching. Have you heard the one about the Ten Commandments, which God uses like a chain link fence to hem you in? This is taught by those who perceive the commands of God as something to fence you in rather than something to be written on your heart to set you free. In contrast, if I follow the Spirit of God and He sets my heart free from adultery, I will not have to follow a rule to keep my flesh under control. The truth of the Scripture is made alive in my heart by the Holy Spirit, and my flesh dies to the sinful desire. This is true salvation.

A few years ago I had the opportunity to hear one of the nation's most highly respected and honored youth ministers speak. He strongly asserted that the Bible is like a stake in the ground that men use to shackle elephants. He was emphatic that biblical principles would chain young people to religion to keep them from running away. As God is my witness, this is what is being taught to the youth of this generation. But actually, he makes my point for me. Because men erroneously use the Bible as a rule book, it *has* become a chain of bondage to them. This was never God's intent. The Bible was intended to be used as a tool to draw you into a very faithful relationship of obeying *Jesus* – not a book. But were it not for the religious rule, a Pharisee would have nothing to be faithful to. Though they may look straight at you with convincing eyes and say that they are following a principle of wisdom – I say if it looks like a chained elephant, and walks like a chained elephant . . . it's a chained elephant.

For my next point, I would like to kill two birds with one stone. The first bird is the aggressive tendency of Pharisees to force their rules on you; the second is the legalistic rule of praying over a meal. Nothing seems to raise the indignation of pious pretenders quite like starting to eat without praying – head bowed, and eyes closed. At the religious college I attended, the pressure to pray over meals was so intense that even those students who lived in *open* sin felt compelled to go through the motions. To them it was – fake a prayer, or suffer the wrath of the Pharisees. Now you would think that the religious, who purport a relationship with God, would want people to be honest. But in reality, legalistically following the 'spiritual' rules has become far more paramount to them than sincerity. And much like Eve, pushing their sin onto someone else always seems to be a high priority.

Now don't misunderstand me, there is nothing wrong with praying over your meal, but *why* do you do it? Honestly. Is it because you are being led by the Spirit of God in the moment, or is it because of a man made rule that says so? Even churches go through the motions and practice shallow token prayers to open and close their services. And why do they do it? What is their motive? Religious obligation. Most ministers wouldn't dare close a service without praying – because rules run deep. Break them and you are sure to suffer the consequences. I encourage you, however, to pray as you feel the guidance of God lead you to pray, and refuse to pray a shallow token prayer over any meal or church service just because some religious concept bullies you to.

The common Pharisee is very skilled at training the naïve to blindly follow such religious concepts. Once indoctrinated, the new student becomes so programmed that he can be likened to a pious Pavlov's dog. Ivan Pavlov was a Russian physiologist who studied reflex behavior, and used dogs in his experiments. Each time he fed the dogs, he rang a bell. He did this so many times, the dogs became accustomed to the bell. Then one day, he didn't feed them – he just rang the bell. What happened? The dogs began salivating. A religious Pavlov's dog, therefore, is one who is trained to give a conditioned response when found in certain circumstances. Ring the bell of 'works' and watch any possibility of a deep conversation about *good* works be rejected. Ring the bell of hearing God and watch the 'God doesn't speak to everybody' program kick in. And God forbid you ring the bell of 'salvation is more than just praying the sinner's prayer.' They won't salivate – they'll bare their teeth.

Under the guise of maintaining doctrinal purity, Pharisees have managed to manufacture their 'Christianity' into one conditioned response after another – far removed from a heart relationship with God. And they are so ingrained in denial that they have become insulated from reality. Potential followers are no longer trained in the truth, but rather trained to outright reject any statement that questions their belief structure. They have become soul-less, mechanized robots that react in each moment according to their programming. You see, it is easier to act right, than be right; it is easier to act like a follower, than to be a follower. How effective is the pharisaical indoctrination? Jesus says that the new false converts of the Pharisees are "twice as much the son of hell" as they are (Matthew 23:15).

Ultimately, validation and self-justification are the legalistic end alls for the actions of a Pharisee. Because he accepts certain beliefs, he considers himself to be right with God; because he does certain noble works, he considers himself a good person; and because he obeys *selective* Scripture verses, he considers himself an obedient follower. These are called 'do to be' actions. I 'do' *this action* – insert the appropriate prayer, sincere deed, or cause – and therefore I must 'be' *this way*. But God's ancient path is not a journey that consists of changing the outward to validate the inward. No, God alters our inward being, putting the self to death, and that in turn affects the actions of the outward man.

It is this obsession with the outward, however, that claims the attention of the Pharisee. When you add a self-created outward perception to a self-created determination, the outcome is 'judgment.' To judge is to *tell yourself* what is true or false; to determine within your own understanding what is right or wrong. It is a man-made discernment deficient of the voice of God. We are instructed by Jesus Himself not to judge, for the standard in which you judge others will be measured back to you (Matthew 7:1). You see, man was never meant to discern based on his own understanding; he was created to hear and rely on God's discernment. Jesus drove this point home when He stated, "Do not judge according to appearance, but judge with righteous judgment" (John 7:24).

Righteous judgment. This is not some pharisaical conclusion based on a legalistic understanding of Scripture or the traditions of men. No, Jesus commands us to judge righteously. This means that any determination, discernment, or conclusion that a follower of God comes to must be centered solely on the voice of God. To be credited as righteous, one must faith. To faith, one must hear the spoken word of God. Therefore, to make any spiritual determination *righteously* requires the truth to be revealed by God. Even the Apostle Paul declared that he didn't judge himself because he couldn't know anything about himself on his own – it was the Lord who judged him (I Corinthians 4:3-5).

To see if you understand, let's have a pop quiz! If you get the answer right you get a thousand points; if you get it wrong you have to go back and start over at Chapter 1☺. Ready? Individual A tells person X that person X is in sin because of person X's outward actions. Individual B tells person X that he is in sin because of a Scripture verse. Individual C tells person X that he is in sin because God spoke and revealed the truth about his heart. Now, who is judging unrighteously and who is not? Answer: Individual A is judging unrighteously because he based his perception on the outward appearance, not on the truth of the heart revealed by God. Individual B is judging unrighteously because he based his perception legalistically on his own understanding of the Scripture instead of the voice of God. But individual C is not judging unrighteously because he based his perception on God's perception, on the truth revealed by the Spirit.

It all comes down to the source from which you draw.

Here's a bonus question: Which person should person X listen to? Okay, it's a trick question, but the answer is telling. Technically, he shouldn't listen to any of them. He should listen to God. But that being said, if individual C is hearing and speaking from God, person X will be held accountable to hear God through him – and he should listen with open ears.

This false concept of judging has become so prevalent today that true followers of God are accosted any time they speak out in obedience. Most religious people, however, refuse to speak any truth whatsoever for fear of being labeled with the 'j' word. As I have pointed out in churches before, if we can't tell someone that they are lost because it is 'judging,' then what are we doing here? Shut down the church and close the doors – we won't help anyone anyway.

This concept of man's judgment brings up the question: Have you ever met Shirley God? You know, when you are discussing deep spiritual issues with a Pharisee who – instead of seeking God – declares . . . *surely God.* Surely God would want me to . . . surely God wouldn't want me to . . . and the judgment of man then triumphs over the actual will of God. Why not just ask God? Because to ask God would require seeking and waiting on Him to speak, and most likely cause the need for repentance to rear its ugly head. But, surely God understands how hard it is to follow him, right? Sorry, God's name is not Shirley.

Though the sign at the Pharisee's gate spells out 'Christian,' this kingdom of flimsy walls was built all for self. He blows his own horn to announce the amazing ministry opportunities given him and the 'good' works that he has accomplished for God. A good Pharisee will labor so hard in the flesh to appear a pious servant of God that he will actually deceive himself and become proud of his 'humility.'

These religious kings spend the day doing other important self-centered kingdom business as well. From telling themselves that they are right with God, to picking and choosing which truth to accept or reject. The work is unending in the effort to make sure every preconceived perception is justified by at least one Scripture reference, established doctrine, or popular tradition. And to them it is worth the effort. The last thing they want to do is be embarrassed in front of all the other Pharisees.

So in his own little, make-believe world, the Pharisee practices his craft. He names and claims as many promises as he can in order to 'be blessed,' though God never spoke any of them to him. With a stuffy nose he chants his positive confessions to ward off the evils of sickness, never admitting that God requires honesty in his confessions. And if he thinks he can force you to listen to him by blocking your TV, turning off your radio, or ganging up on you with several of his friends, he will do it. After all, it's his fantasy, and here he is the 'prophet of God.' So he can tell people that they have to listen to him if he wants to. The sad thing is – many do.

> *Rightly did Isaiah prophesy of you hypocrites, as*
> *it is written: This people honors me with their*
> *lips, but their heart is far from me. But in vain do*
> *they worship me, teaching as doctrines the*
> *precepts of men. Neglecting the commandment of*
> *God, you hold to the tradition of men.*
> *Mark 7:6-8*

Should you confront these deceived deceivers, be prepared for a battle. To them you are not helping them to see the truth. On the contrary, you are attacking their very way of life. When you tell them what God is speaking, you are calling into question their validation. You see, these doctrines are life to them. Since they lack any real relationship with God, if you knock down their house of cards you are in effect knocking down their god. If they don't have these false doctrines, they are lost. And losing their souls for the truth is not what they signed up for.

Although speaking the unveiled reality of God defeats every argument, a Pharisee will blindly defend his flawed position because deep down inside he is defending self. Oh, how the flesh will war to stay alive and be right in its own eyes.

From emotional outbursts to strange rules to argue by, there is no counting the ways the self will wrangle to be justified. The more the flesh screams in anger and offense, the more proof there is that the truth is doing its work.

This flesh reaction is sad really when you come to realize just how much effort Pharisees put into making sure that their chains of bondage don't rattle. If they can keep them quiet, they presume that they are 'set free.' But push them and cause the chains to rattle – and they will blame you for the sin that rushes out of their hearts. You are now labeled an instigator of mischief, mean spirited, and holier than thou.

One day my friend Joe and I had a discussion with a modern-day Pharisee fresh out of Bible school. This self-secure young man firmly held the belief that God doesn't speak to most men, let alone continually to all as we believe. So, in the conversation we pointed out that Jesus said His sheep hear His voice (John 10:27). Now this puts a religious person in a serious dilemma. Would he reject years of false indoctrination by beloved and respected men? Would he be willing to admit that God does speak, and prove the reality that he was not one of Jesus' sheep? We had hoped so. But this young upstart chose instead to argue against the Scripture, the voice of God, and all reason. After a short discussion and several feinted smiles, he slowly became unraveled, and the sound of his chains jingled. It was then that his undelivered flesh lashed out.

The onslaught is the typical fare. An obviously false position is justified by 2,000 years of tradition and the firm agreement of a multitude of misled ministers. The narrow road to salvation is then sufficiently broadened so the undelivered can be allowed in. Next comes the verbal assault of name calling, insults, and the old 'accuse the accuser.' That's when the flesh really erupts with an attempt to intimidate physically by standing up. With fists clinched and arms flailing, all logic is forsaken. Then out come the labels – and my personal favorite – 'you're a cult!' The obvious next step is executed and performed flawlessly – storming out of the house with self-justification firmly intact. Follow all this up with multiple argumentative e-mails, and you have a typical pharisaical reaction to the truth. And all this because he just didn't want to admit that God speaks.

Regardless of the battleground or the topic, Cain will always attack Abel. Those who are in the flesh will always persecute those born of the Spirit (Galatians 4:29). It's just the way it is. And the Pharisee is the poster boy for self-righteous persecution. He may wear the very latest in sheep's clothing fashion, but inevitably he will bare his fangs if he fears he will be discovered. Pretense and self-deception have become what it means for the Pharisee to follow God, and the threat of confrontation is his defense. I pray you will see past the intimidation and hold on to the truth that God reveals to you.

Well, the time has come. It is time for you to take an honest look in the mirror. When you gaze deeply into the mirror of your soul, what do you see staring back at you? Who are you? Do you see a Pharisee? Be very careful here. It is so very easy to taint your perception with you. The yeast of hypocrisy is ever willing to contaminate reality with its poison. A clear and honest singular perception is what you need right now to see the truth and to choose the right path. But which path will you choose: follower or Pharisee? So to help, let me pose a question.

Do you dance? Now, tell me when you get that confused look off your face so we can continue. Ready? Elijah asked the people, "How long will you hesitate between two opinions?" (I Kings 18:21). The Hebrew for hesitate means to skip over, to limp, to dance.[1] So, I ask the question again, do *you* dance? Are you dancing back and forth between living wholeheartedly and living as a religious Pharisee? Do you wavier instead of being fully persuaded by God's influence on your life? There is only one narrow, ancient path to follow, and if you don't remain true to it you will never reach the journey's end.

The remedy to dancing is often found within the resolve. Paul said that he did not vacillate in his intentions so that there was never "yes, yes and no, no at the same time" (II Corinthians 1:17). The Greek word for "intend" has within its meaning – to resolve.[2] Paul did not dance because he was resolved. His mind and his heart were convinced so that there was no hesitation in his walk with God. Please realize that Paul wasn't just convincing himself – he was convinced *by God*. He had been a Pharisee, but no more.

It is a very real resolution – be a Pharisee who only pretends to know the Living God – or be a follower who actually does. And unless you declare atheism, you will have to make a choice. But of what real value is it to be tossed back and forth by indecision? Why be caught in the struggle of seeing the truth, but then letting your self-interest sway you from the path that follows God? James 1:6-8 points out that anyone not trusting the wisdom of God is like a man tossed by the sea, double-minded and unstable in *all* his ways. The word "tossed" denotes moving to and fro, to agitate.[3] Not trusting the voice of God when He reveals the truth will result in a spiritual agitation, proving just how unstable and unsettled you are. And II Peter 3:16 points out that it is the unstable who distort the Scriptures. So why hesitate? Why claim to live one way, only to live another? A double-minded dancer who tries to pirouette in the middle of the road is going to get hit. There is massacre in the middle.

If you are not following God with *all* of your heart, then why are you rejecting Him? It is of no value before God when you "profess to know God" but then by your actions "deny Him" (Titus 1:16). Such an unholy alliance with self-justified compromise is nothing more than a direct denunciation of the heart of God. So ask yourself the hard question: Do I have the mettle to live so that the mirror reflects the divinity of God rather than the sinful stain of my flesh? As always, it is your choice to live complacently in compromise or to aggressively seek agreement with God's unveiled reality.

Purify your hearts you double-minded (James 4:8), and learn to become steadfast and immovable so that your toil is not in vain (I Corinthians 15:58). Outright reject the pharisaical lifestyle and choose to become a true follower of God so you can say with a vengeance, "I have trusted without wavering" (Psalm 26:1). The choice to follow is yours – and yours alone.

Application Summary

God, in His mercy, has given you the free will to reject Him or to follow Him. He will even allow you to become a Pharisee and play a religious game – if you so choose. If you do decide to live a 'spiritual' self-righteous and undelivered life, you will be nothing more than an unchristian 'Christian.' All of your religious dealings and well-meaning actions will only be self-initiated works that you have tacked God's name onto. You may even become quite zealous in your uninformed and misperceived spirituality. But of what real value is a self-indulging code of conduct that is covered by a shroud of piety? Pretense will never help you become delivered from your self, nor will it help you find the God who desires complete honesty from His children.

When you look in the mirror – do you find your 'self'? Do you find your 'self' religiously balking at the truth that stings by turning to a reasoned self-justification? Do you find your 'self' shoring up your spiritual failings by whitewashing them so you don't have to be truly honest? Do you find your 'self' following religious rules to feel justified that somehow you really are a Christian?

Legalism kills any true chance of relationship with the Father. Even the well-intentioned pursuit of Scripture verses will not help unless they teach you to follow Christ instead of a book. And pushing other people to follow your self-determined rules will not make *them* more spiritual nor will it validate *you*. It will just add sin unto sin.

Are you a spiritual Pavlov's dog? Not taught to follow the voice of the Living God in every moment, but taught to blindly follow a well-conceived set of religious doctrines? Have you studied these supposed 'truths' under the guidance of God, or do you accept them because deep down inside your trust is actually in man? If you believe that you are validated as genuine because you follow a majority view that has been labeled 'biblical' – you are nothing more than a Pharisee.

When you decide what is right or wrong – what exactly do you base it on? Do you base your judgment on the facts and available information or maybe even your perception of sound biblical principles? This type of judging is not from the voice of God and therefore unrighteous. Righteous judgment comes from what God reveals – not your own tainted perceptions.

When you find yourself in various spiritual discussions, have you allowed God to deliver you from the influence of self? Or do you try to weasel your way out of the truth by saying, "Let's just agree to disagree?" Maybe you are a Pharisee that justifies your sin with statements like, "Well, nobody's perfect" or "I'm just a sinner saved by grace." And if I spiritually push you so hard that your chains of bondage rattle, will you revert to intimidation, name calling, and insults? Cain will always attack Abel just as a Pharisee will always attack the followers of God. And there is nothing anyone can do about it.

Look in the mirror. What do you see? Are you willing to see the truth and allow God to have His way over your complete being? Trying to play both sides of the fence by dancing back and forth is foolish. There is nothing but massacre in the middle of the road. You must pick a side.

If you choose to follow, you will have nothing to do with the hollow practice of going through the motions. A follower refuses to play religious games that are vain and empty because he wants a deep, genuine relationship with his God. Therefore, I pray that you will reject the pharisaical lifestyle of religious bondage, and instead learn to follow God in every area of your life – and to do it without wavering.

Challenging Your Perception

1. Have you been preconditioned by men to react out of 'habit' rather than hearing God in the moment? Are you able to recognize the difference between following God and following spiritual principles?

2. Are *you* a Pharisee? Do you find that you have to convince yourself that you are not a Pharisee every time the chains of your bondage rattle?

3. Are you willing to see the teeth of a wolf dressed up in a young man's suit and tie, in a middle-aged woman's modest dress, and in an elderly woman's shawl? Are you willing to remove the wool that has been pulled over the eyes of your heart? Will you be a follower or a Pharisee?

Endnotes

1. James Strong, LL.D., S.T.D., *The New Strong's Exhaustive Concordance of the Bible*, Dictionary of the Hebrew Bible, copyright 1990 by Thomas Nelson Publishers, page 95, Hebrew #6452, *pawsakh*.
2. Spiros Zodhiates, TH.D., *The Complete Word Study Dictionary New Testament*, D/B/A AMG Publishers, copyright 1992 by Spiros Zodhiates and AMG International Inc., page 346, Greek #1011, *bouleuso*.
3. Ibid., page 1263, Greek #4494, *rhipiso*.

Repentance is a full-blooded, wholehearted, uncompromising renunciation of one's former attitude and outlook. It is a change of heart that always results in a change of course.

Arthur Wallis

There is no improving the future without disturbing the present.

William Booth

When you speak of total abandon, people accuse you of being fanatical and unbalanced. This is because they don't want to completely die to their own desires.

Fenelon

Only the man who is dead to his own will can follow Christ.

Dietrich Bonhoeffer

Chapter

12

BE THE EXCEPTION
(If Not You, Who?)

"For the eyes of the Lord move to and fro throughout the earth that He may strongly support those whose heart is completely His."
II Chronicles 16:9

We last left our hero with a choice. Who will he choose to be? Will he follow the newly discovered ancient way of living that clearly affects his heart so deeply? Or will he forsake such uncommon understanding for the far more common life of comfort and familiarity? Actually, the conclusion of this story is unfinished – left for you to write. For you are the hero, or at least could be. Maybe you are only starting to find the ancient path that has been obscured by thousands of years of overgrowth. It is also possible that you have been on the path for some time and are just now beginning to really hear the call to a deeper way of life. Or maybe you find yourself considering compromise; questioning if this newly discovered life is worth the cost and sacrifice. Regardless, you now stand confronted with the truth and must decide where you will choose to 'live.' Will you be a religious bystander, or will you be the hero God wants you to be?

 CRBVECRCRBVECRCRBVECRCRBVECRCRBVECRCRBV

The hardest part of waking up in the morning is letting your eyes adjust to the light. It takes a little time for the discomfort to subside, but when it does, the pain goes away and all is clearly visible. I encourage you to awaken from any shadowy slumber that has darkened your eyes from perceiving the truth. Recognize the influence of God on your life even now that is drawing you to find Him. It is strange that so many continue to stare into darkness fully convinced that they have sight. Don't let this be true of you. I implore you, I beseech you: Be the Exception! Be the anomaly! Be unique and have in mind the things of God rather than the desires of men. Be that rare Exception who is willing to open your eyes and see.

As we have discussed previously, the main verse for this book is Jeremiah 6:16 in which we are exhorted to "Stand by the ways and see. . ." Are you now able to stand back with a focused and untainted gaze and see past the obvious? Are you able to distinguish between the religiously worthless and the spiritually valuable? I truly hope so. And if you are developing a healthy perception, it's okay if you don't have everything all figured out. After all, who does? The fact is that you still don't know what you don't know. But thankfully, God will be faithful to continue to help you avoid the darkness that would so deceptively lead you astray.

Do you see the deception of the non-Christian 'Christianity' that prays *at* God instead of *to* God? Do you see the fallacy of placing your faith in the fact that you prayed the sinner's prayer? Can you now understand the error of believing that you are saved because you accept the factual reality of Jesus' life, death, and resurrection – or because after you were baptized the preacher said so? Are you now aware of how the cross has been stripped of its power because so few want it to be an instrument of death to self? Is it acceptable to you that in this generation you can 'receive Jesus' without Jesus receiving you? That it has become common place to 'take up your cross' without ever dying to sin and self? That songs are sung in church services around the world that proclaim "I surrender all," only to actually mean "I surrender some"?

Don't settle for the compromise that cowers in the corner. Don't settle for the cliché Sunday school pat answers that contradict the truth. Of what value is a conditioned response that is used to excuse spiritual ignorance? And why settle for the lie of positive confession; do you actually think God wants us to be deceitful? Just confess *honestly* before God; that is the heart He desires of you.

Remember to avoid, at all costs, the practice of pretense. God sees all. And if you try to hide your chains of bondage behind a mask of make-believe, it is just a matter of time before your flesh will sneak out from behind it. Beware the deceptiveness of this half-hearted hypocrisy. It is capable of growing out of control to the degree that it completely blinds you. Rather than duplicity, God desires a whole heart laid bare before Him – one that is willing to walk in all truthfulness.

Jeremiah's next point in 6:16 is that you should "ask for the ancient paths." Finding the way to God will require spiritual hunger and passion for Him. Turn to God and solicit help from Him in every step. When you seek the face of God, you can't settle for 'I guess so' or 'I hope so.' Engage God with heart – heart first, heart only, and heart always. Make your goal to walk with God according to the Spirit (Romans 8:5), and know that the word Jesus speaks to you *is* that Spirit (John 6:63). This is how you should walk the path of God to discover the honest truth and find real rest for your soul.

The title verse for this chapter is II Chronicles 16:9:

For the eyes of the Lord move to and fro
throughout the earth that He may strongly support
those whose heart is completely His.

This verse should encourage you to the depths of your being. You see, as you search down the ancient path to know the Living God – the Living God is searching for *you* too. Simply amazing! It is the Lord's purpose, not only to find you, but to strengthen you, so boast of your weakness that the power of Christ may dwell in you (II Corinthians 12:9). Since the Lord looks upon those who are contrite and tremble at His spoken word (Isaiah 66:2) – be broken before Him and give weight to what He speaks to you. In this know that you don't have to be alone in this world, for God "longs to be gracious to you . . . He waits on high to have compassion on you" (Isaiah 30:18). Do you see how absolutely valuable it is to have a heart that is completely given to God?

God's changing influence of grace in your life is to deliver you from all worldliness. He is teaching you to "deny ungodliness" (Titus 2:12). But you will not be able to harvest this fruit of right relationship unless you first plow up your "fallow ground" (Jeremiah 4:3). When your heart becomes broken and willing to accept the seed of His spoken word (Matthew 13:23), God will cause His word to germinate within your heart. Then, when His voice is bearing fruit in your life – you *will* say no to ungodliness and live righteously before Him. It is even possible to mature in Christ to the point that you would no longer require another person to instruct you. Imagine growing so close to the Father that "you have no need for anyone to teach you" (I John 2:27). Now that's what I call a relationship.

To whom will God speak and give warning (Jeremiah 6:10)? He will speak to you if you are willing. But understand that deep calls to deep (Psalm 42:7), so don't be shallow in your hearing. Have ears to hear. Desire to know the truth – even if it hurts. God's word to you is for your good; don't reject it because your flesh dislikes death.

Learn to trust the voice of God deeply. Your faith in Him will never be a mistake. But you must trust. God is solid and reliable in His purpose for you. The Scripture repeatedly compares the Lord to the strongest of rocks. He is dependable and true to His word. Be the Exception that willingly lays everything out before God – for you will never be disappointed.

Everyone hears God – whether they want to admit it or not. The difference is that it is only the Exception who becomes righteous because he puts his full faith in the voice of God. Don't be like the Pharisee who turns a relationship with God into some sort of contractual agreement validated by following rules, precepts, or biblical principles. This is not faith. Legalism tries to be okay by doing instead of being. *Be* right with God by trusting His voice to the point of complete obedience. And you will be determined right with God when *He* says so. This is heart – this is following God.

"Woe to him who builds a house without righteousness" (Jeremiah 22:13). For if the house of your life isn't built by trusting to the point that you practice what God speaks to you, your house built on sand will fall (Matthew 7:26-27). Therefore, know that you are laboring in vain if the Lord is not the one who is actively constructing your 'house' (Psalm 127:1). If you don't learn what this means, you will stand before God on that day only to find that the arm of man has failed you entirely.

Prepare your heart for the influence of God. Make the paths of your heart straight for Him (Matthew 3:3). When the Spirit of God wants to help you, He shouldn't have to bob and weave around the obstacles of self that hinder His path to the center of your heart. Humble yourself and lower every mountain of self-glory, while raising up every valley of self-loathing. The goal is to make the rough ground of your heart level (Isaiah 40:4). And with God's help, you can also have straight paths for *your feet* to walk upon (Hebrews 12:13).

Don't just say you are repentant – anyone can do that. Instead, show fruit of your repentance (Luke 3:8), and prove your repentance by your deeds (Acts 26:20). But this must come from an inner change. So, don't try to do better – try to see better. When you repent and God changes your perception, you will be able to see as He sees. The outward things of this world will lose their luster. And when they become less valuable in your eyes, you will be unwilling to separate yourself from God to possess them.

As you walk the ancient path, let God fully discipline you to the point that you become established, with your feet firmly on the ground. Then there will be no need to add to or take away from anything God reveals to you (Deuteronomy 4:2). In this same way, learn not to rush forward or to shrink back. God is always aware of where you are – there's no need to get jumpy.

I encourage you to own a salvation that produces genuine deliverance from self and sin. You don't have to stay the same anymore. You do not have to live with your flesh out of control – you can be delivered from it. It is of no use trying to contain your self-love in some sort of religious Ziploc® bag, thinking that you can seal it in so it won't leak out. It will eventually escape in one way or another. Instead, pour yourself out completely and throw away the bag. When you are delivered, you will have no need to conceal the flesh – it will be dead.

If you are still hung up on the mistaken concept that you have to sin every day, understand how that mindset comes from a heart swayed by the dominion of sin. Just as it is true that a person may be far from God and completely separated from Him, so a person is capable, with the Lord's help, of walking right next to Him continually. Sin is separation by choice. Although you had no choice when you were tainted by self and alienated from the Father at birth, it is your choice now. Therefore it is up to you: Do you want a real salvation, or just a plastic facsimile?

When you are truly saved from your sin, you will no longer have a tendency to sin. Your tendency will be to hear and trust the voice of God and to walk in obedience to His Spirit. Since everything that is not from faith is sin that separates you from God (Romans 14:23), it will no longer be acceptable to you to reject the voice from which that faith comes. You will no longer be willing to accept a half-hearted, undelivered existence lived under the guise of religion. The need to follow religious rules and traditions in order to justify a false salvation will fade away. When you love and trust God with all your heart, you *will be saved*; you will be changed and will actually be set free from the self that separates you from Him.

God's kindness and patience will grant you repentance if that is what you truly desire. But don't take this for granted – rather be quick to repent and humble of heart. Then let repentance do its work. Allow repentance to fully change the way you perceive the value of the things around you. If you fully surrender to the changes God desires of you, you will soon discover what it means to walk in repentance daily. Walk out a delivered life with God and put to shame those who claim it can't be done.

As you grow closer to the Father, allow God to deliver you from a guilty conscience. Hanging on to the guilt of past issues after God has cleansed you of them will only do you harm. By "Keeping faith and a good conscience" you will avoid the possibility of shipwrecking your faith (I Timothy 1:19). So trust what God tells you about you. Anything else is mere speculation on your part.

There are multitudes of religious organizations that declare inaccurately that once you have been saved, you have all of God that there is to have. Wicked. They say this because they don't want to be responsible to seek deeper. By the way, these are the same men who declare that you can be born again without being spiritually reborn, that repentance is just being sincerely sorry, and who tell you 'God doesn't speak that way.' Trust *them* if you wish, but I'd rather hear and trust the reality of God. God is so much higher, deeper, and wiser than us (Isaiah 55:9) – to say there is no 'more' screams heresy. If God wants to give you a deeper understanding, a deeper heart connection to Him, or a deeper spirit that overflows with power and boldness – don't be foolish – let Him.

Speaking of 'more,' from the very beginning of your relationship, God works to create in you a mature heart. Many Bible translations translate that He wants us to be 'perfect' (Matthew 5:48), which causes some to think He means 'flawless.' Actually, the word generally means to be complete, mature, reaching an intended goal.[1] And what is that goal? God shapes His children into the image of His Son (Romans 8:29). We are to be like Christ. God labors to make us complete so that we are able to move from loving Him with all *we* know – to loving Him with all *He* knows. Yes, there is more of God – and He gives more to those who desire Him.

Also, let me encourage you to make sure that you don't get caught up in the thought of being an Exception. Rather, let your enthusiasm be found in the fact that God is real, that He speaks, and that He is actively revealing His will. In this way you can focus on the reality that all things come from God, all things are done through God, and all glory goes to God (Romans 11:36). Not you.

If you are an Exception, and choose to find and follow God in the truth, I hope you will be able to be part of a genuine fellowship. The value of being with others who have died to themselves and have chosen to trust the voice of the Living God wholeheartedly is immeasurable. In a true community of believers, the people are of one heart and one mind in full agreement with the Spirit of God. The leadership has no agenda other than complete obedience to God. Waiting on Him to speak is not a chore to be avoided, it is a choice done with passion and heart. Now I realize that in this day and age it may feel like a daunting task to find a genuine body of Christ. But remember what Jesus said, "For where two or three have gathered together in My name, I am there in their midst" (Matthew 18:20). So you don't need a crowd to experience true community, just one other true believer. If you are unable to find even one, consider Abraham – he walked alone with his God, and he came out okay.

The sad reality is that there are numerous Harlot Churches muddying the spiritual landscape. They are controlled by little kings of religion who build their church palaces in competition with each other. Yes, the whore projects the illusion of community, the illusion of fruit – but nothing more. Honesty and truth are not in her. How can the nations come to her light (Isaiah 60:3) if they can't stop laughing at her half-built tower (Luke 14:29)? But the harlot drowns out the laughter with the accolades of her lovers. So let the whitewashed self-important enjoy their sin for a season. It will end. Truly I say to you – they have their reward.

Are you now able to hear the 'call to suffer'? Are you now able to understand Paul's sobering invitation – "Join with me in suffering for the gospel" (II Timothy 1:8)? The reality of the uncontrolled flesh of men – particularly of the religious – brings to light the grave possibility of affliction at their hands. Since "all who desire to live godly in Christ Jesus will be persecuted" (II Timothy 3:12), it is highly recommended that you equip yourself with a mind to suffer (I Peter 4:1). In this, know that 'sticks and stones' may indeed break your bones – but they should never break your spirit. And whatever foul speech is flung your way, do not bother yourself with the taunts of men (I Peter 3:16). As a matter of fact, Jesus said, "Woe to you when all men speak well of you, for this is how their fathers treated the false prophets" (Luke 6:26). So only care about what God thinks; He's the only one who matters.

Do not try to avoid the hatred of this world. Jesus *promised* that, "You will be hated by all" (Matthew 10:22). But know that the hatred of the world was vented at Him long before it was vented at you (John 15:18). Therefore, be like Christ and scorn the shame that is hurled at you (Hebrews 12:2). Be willing to stand – alone if necessary. And if it is God's desire to allow you to become the target of men's hatred, be the Exception who shares in the suffering of Christ on behalf of the church (Colossians 1:24).

Few in this world will lay down their lives and be a willing fool for Christ's sake (I Corinthians 4:10). Ostracism is highly likely and suffering is a biblical promise. So, it may seem only natural to fear what you may have to suffer, but don't. The affliction that men deal out really is momentary and light compared to eternity (II Corinthians 4:17). Rather, "Be faithful unto death" and God "will give you the crown of life" (Revelation 2:10).

I once heard Leonard Ravenhill ask:

> *If not here, where?*
> *If not now, when?*
> *If not you, who?*

Do *you* hear the trumpet call to war? If so, it is time to be fearless. It is time for you to show that you are made of sterner stuff. Although this war is not a battle against flesh and blood (Ephesians 6:12), it can be very taxing. It is, therefore, good to be filled with the indignation of God (Psalm 119:53), and to walk with the zeal of Phinehas (Numbers 25:6-13). You may even be required to toss some tables of your own one day (Matthew 21:12). But if so, make sure your actions are never according to the flesh. *Know* that your actions are based solely on the voice of God – and absolutely nothing else.

Don't glorify spiritual battle; it's just something that has to be done. When reality sets in, you will see just how difficult it can be. That being said, you are not called to the spiritual battlefield by God to be a bystander. The sword that you carry is the spoken word of God (Ephesians 6:17), so be attentive to His voice at all times. Be aware that this weapon is quite sharp (Hebrews 4:12), and offends easily (Jeremiah 6:10). Let the word of God do its work; let the sword of the Spirit draw spiritual blood (Jeremiah 48:10). God knows that it cuts and offends – that's what the sword is for.

Realize that you don't have to battle according to the rules of men. Though they may argue based on intellect, position, or pay grade – don't fall for it. Many will attempt to debate using manmade theology from various schools of thought, but it means little. Most Bible students are taught nothing more than how to parrot back the teachings of men, anyway. They may glory on their 'education,' but they are not trained in how to hear God and die to themselves. You may even feel compelled to try to justify yourself before them. Don't. You don't have to prove anything to anyone – just listen to God and trust what He tells you. Oh, and feel free to wreck the moment. You know, breaking those social rules of men? Jesus wrecked several nice mealtimes – even when invited to the houses of very important people (Luke 11:37-52). Then at other times, Jesus was silent when the religious wanted Him to speak (John 8:3-6, Matthew 26:63). You see, there are no rules – only the leadership of the Holy Spirit in the moment.

Be the servant of God who is willing to free others from the chains of self that are dragging them to hell. The Lord will be with you, and will reveal to you other Exceptions who need help. Now, it may seem like you are looking for a needle in a hay stack, but just follow God – He will lead you. You can be the voice that cries out in the wilderness to them (John 1:23), so do so boldly. As you speak the honest truth in love (Ephesians 4:15), the sound will resonate in every heart that is seeking the ancient path to God.

Value discipleship. First your own; then others. To disciple even one true follower of God is worth a lifetime, so don't look down on the day of small beginnings (Zechariah 4:10). The fact is – God likes to grow large trees from very small seeds. But, realize you cannot take a person any deeper than you yourself have gone. So go deep. Train them to die to self daily in complete surrender. Help them to perceive the voice of God and to trust Him with all their heart.

As you teach others, keep your shoulder to the door. By that I mean, beware of false followers. They can infiltrate and suck the life out of a vital fellowship quickly. If they don't really want to surrender all and really don't want to be delivered from their self – then what are they doing there? Their motive is suspect, and if God has called you to shepherd a flock, it will be your responsibility to test every spirit (I John 4:1). Therefore be accountable before God and guard the trust. Remove the wolves from the fold as led by the Spirit. When Jesus taught on earth, He thinned the crowd on several occasions – and He still does it today.

Always give God the opportunity to speak. Give Him a chance to say yes or no, or to take you in a completely different direction if He wants to. Even when you 'know that you know' – the Spirit may show you a nuance of truth you have never perceived before. So don't let arrogance or presumption brush-off the instrument through which the Lord chooses to speak. God determines the mouthpiece, you just be the ear.

Know that it is never wrong to test yourself to see if you are actively trusting the voice of God (II Corinthians 13:5). Be willing to examine yourself openly before God – He will show you any areas that you are deficient. During this process, be broken and contrite. The illumination that God desires to reveal to you is difficult to see if you are full of your 'self' and your flesh blocks the light.

No longer can you just believe what men tell you, or just believe what you read. You need to "study to show yourself approved" (II Timothy 2:15 KJV). Be noble minded and actually search the Scriptures to know the truth (Acts 17:11). Don't ignore the proper definitions of words – or worse, alter them just to protect your pet doctrines. Much harm has been done to the Scriptures because of the spiritual slothfulness of past generations.

If you have found your way to read this entire book, I have high hopes for you. I encourage you to continue seeking God with all your heart. Be the Exception. Be the one who hears and trusts the Living God. Be the one who rejects this world and sacrifices all for His kingdom. Be the servant of God who the world is not worthy of (Hebrews 11:38). And join with me in rebuilding the ancient ruins that have long been disregarded by men (Isaiah 61:4). I pray that whatever corner of this planet you travel to, God finds you seeking Him.

Well, we are at the end of our time together. So let us ponder one final thought. Is all this *really* possible? Does God really live and speak and influence mankind? Is it possible to hear and trust the voice of God in complete wholehearted obedience? Can we experience a salvation that actually delivers us from the bondage of daily sin? And is there really a way for us to walk in relationship with God in the cool of the evening as Adam did? Absolutely. For I testify to you that I have found the ancient path and have walked it with my own two feet. And so can you. If your heart cries out for God, He will answer you. Search the Scriptures for the hidden truth and meditate on the realities God reveals to you. Learn what it means to lay down your life. Learn what it means to live in complete honesty before God without even a hint of hypocrisy. And when you do, and the Father kindles a fire of passion for Him in your heart – shake the very gates of hell. Then pass the flame on to the next generation – don't let it die with you. And know this, you are not alone. God stands with his children. So find God, trust His voice, and die well.

JB

Psalms 139

O Lord, You have searched me and known me.
You know when I sit down and when I rise up;
You understand my thought from afar.
You scrutinize my path and my lying down,
And are intimately acquainted with all my ways.
Even before there is a word on my tongue,
Behold, O Lord, You know it all.
You have enclosed me behind and before,
And laid Your hand upon me.
Such knowledge is too wonderful for me;
It is too high, I cannot attain to it.

Where can I go from Your Spirit?
Or where can I flee from Your presence?
If I ascend to heaven, You are there;
If I make my bed in Sheol, behold, You are there.
If I take the wings of the dawn,
If I dwell in the remotest part of the sea,
Even there Your hand will lead me,
And Your right hand will lay hold of me.
If I say, "Surely the darkness will overwhelm me,
And the light around me will be night,"
Even the darkness is not dark to You,
And the night is as bright as the day.
Darkness and light are alike to You.

For You formed my inward parts;
You wove me in my mother's womb.
I will give thanks to You,
for I am fearfully and wonderfully made;
Wonderful are Your works,
And my soul knows it very well.
My frame was not hidden from You,
When I was made in secret,
And skillfully wrought in the depths of the earth;

Your eyes have seen my unformed substance;
And in Your book were all written
The days that were ordained for me,
When as yet there was not one of them.

How precious also are Your thoughts to me, O God!
How vast is the sum of them!
If I should count them, they would outnumber the sand.
When I awake, I am still with You.

O that You would slay the wicked, O God;
Depart from me, therefore, men of bloodshed.
For they speak against You wickedly,
And Your enemies take Your name in vain.
Do I not hate those who hate You, O Lord?
And do I not loathe those who rise up against You?
I hate them with the utmost hatred;
They have become my enemies.

Search me, O God, and know my heart;
Try me and know my anxious thoughts;
And see if there be any hurtful way in me,
And lead me in the everlasting way.

CRBEUS CRBEUS CRBEUS CRBEUS CRBEUS CRBEU

The world knows nothing of its greatest men.

Henry Taylor

Application Summary

Be the hero, be the Exception.

Endnotes

1. Spiros Zodhiates, TH.D., *The Complete Word Study Dictionary New Testament*, D/B/A AMG Publishers, copyright 1992 by Spiros Zodhiates and AMG International Inc., page 1372, Greek #5056, teleios, (see also Greek #5057, 5048).

APPENDIX

It is possible after you have read this book and have traveled a short distance down the ancient path that you find you have gotten stuck in a rut. A rut is a groove in the road that has been made by its continual use – and if made deep enough may become difficult to get out of. So, this next bit of information I have tucked back here in the appendix for the person searching for a little extra help.

If you are stuck, know that it is because of you – and no one else. You are the one spinning your wheels in the same circle over and over again to no avail. It is easy at times like these to say, "It's not my fault" or "I'm trying but it just doesn't work." These are actually accusations against God. You are saying, in effect, that you've done your part but God hasn't done His. It is because of this very heart attitude that you have become stuck. You blame God when the fault lies within your own heart. So I pose this question: Have you sought God with *ALL* your heart? God promises that if you do, you *will* find Him (Deuteronomy 4:29). So, if you claim that you have tried to find God but can't – I say, "Let God be true, and every man a liar" (Romans 3:4).

Maybe your plea is that all this is just too confusing. Well, when you stand before God on that day, do you think the statement "I was confused" will excuse you for rejecting the understanding that God was trying to grace into your life? God is not a God of confusion (I Corinthians 14:33), therefore, neither God nor His truth is confusing. The fact is: Confusion is caused when *your* tainted double-vision blurs the truth. You need to learn how to let go of your old way of seeing things. But it's your choice – you can cling to your preconceived understanding, or you can choose to let God change your distorted perception. Just don't blame your half-heartedness on the truth because it contradicts with your darkened understanding. The question is:

When the light scatters your darkness, will you focus on the shadows – or will you focus on the light?

Realize also that God is not asking you just to spin your wheels and go through the motions of following His voice. The Lord is not impressed at all by your outward attempts to say the right thing or to act the right way. "Look what I can do!" is how worldly children get their parents' attention, not how you become a child of God. God desires life to flow from the inside out. When Paul taught that we should prove our repentance by our deeds (Acts 26:20), his point was that those deeds should be the outward evidence of an inward change. A life that boasts obedience to Christ should be a life that actually engages and follows Christ – not some invented form of following.

The obvious solution to being stuck in a rut is simply to get out of the vehicle and start walking. Yet the love of the old life will have a tremendous pull on your heart. The vehicle, the *way* you have attempted to be right, is still valuable in your eyes – its frame familiar, and the ride comfortable. This has been your way of traveling your whole life; but it is not God's way of traveling. Leave the wreck where it sits, and learn to follow God without dependence on little religious formulas that have no value in delivering you from your self.

As you walk away from these old ways of trying to be right, know that God wants you to get honest with Him. Now it can be very easy to shortcut honesty by re-defining it in your heart to mean 'less-than-honest.' For instance, if a man sees an attractive woman walking down the street and he lusts after her in his heart, his less-than-honest prayer would be: "God, I know that lusting is bad." But if he were to get honest, his prayer would be, "God, I believe that lusting is good." Do you see the difference? The first prayer was a lie because if the man *really* believed lusting was bad, he would not desire it. With his heart and mind convinced, he would be delivered from the pull and influence of lust. But when a man lusts, his thoughts betray him and his actions prove his heart. Thus the honest prayer would be that deep down inside, past all the religious posturing, he actually likes to lust – he thinks it is good. This is honesty. This is the ugly truth. And until you can get this honest with God about whatever your struggle is, you will continue to spin your wheels going nowhere.

Honesty, however, is not what the 'wise' men of this generation teach the gullible. No, they teach that you should develop good habits, to divert your eyes, and to create a mental corral for your desires – and thereby please God outwardly. Do this for six weeks solid they say – and you will be free. But do you see how this is nothing more than another invention of men whereby *you* attempt to deliver *you* by your own willpower – by the arm of your flesh? These religious looking actions are the very boastful works that do not deliver you referred to in Ephesians 2:9.

This concept was a problem for the Exception back in Paul's day as well. He made the point that if you die with Christ, why submit to the worldly rules of "Do not handle, do not taste, do not touch!" (Colossians 2:20-21)? Following self-made, religious rules may have an *appearance* of wisdom, but they have no ability to control the flesh (Colossians 2:23). Being saved is more than a matter of religious compliance. God does not want you to conform to a list of outward religious actions – He wants to change your heart. He wants to change your desires. He wants you to die to your self.

Let's use anger as an example. Let's say you become angry for some reason and choose to apply the acceptable religious action – you hold your tongue. You may even justify your action of bridling your tongue by turning James 1:26 into a rule:

> *If anyone thinks himself to be religious, and yet does not bridle his tongue but deceives his own heart, this man's religion is worthless.*

So, you hold your tongue in a religious attempt to do what you perceive is right. The problem is that James goes on to say that *no one* can tame the tongue (James 3:8). Why? Jesus said, "For out of the overflow of the heart the mouth speaks" (Matthew

12:34 NIV). And now we see the dilemma. It is not the tongue that is angry, or the eye that is lustful – it is the self-centered, self-seeking heart within that values something other than God.

Therefore, being saved is not just acting saved – it is actually being delivered from your sin choices that daily separate you from God. And since it was not God's intention to leave you in bondage to that controlling pull of the flesh, He came to this earth and died on the cross to rescue you. But in order for you to gain personal deliverance, the work of the cross must be applied to your life – not the work of rules. You must follow Jesus' example and die.

Now, dying to self is a painful activity as it requires you to see the truth and let go of all that you know, all that you own, and all that you are. Only God has value, and He will not compete with anyone or anything else. You must learn to see that *He* is God – not you. And in order to see the glory and weight of God clearly – you will need to open your eyes to who you are, to see your sin for what it *really* is.

Jesus said it is the truth you *know* that sets you free (John 8:32). And as previously discussed, the truth is the actual reality of all things unveiled for you by God. Thus, you cannot be set free from your self unless God reveals reality to you: the reality about Him, the reality about you, and the reality about everything in between. But how does that happen? Well, Jesus said God's spoken word is the truth (John 17:17). You must hear and know the truth as God speaks it to you.

It is God's desire to shine light on every angle of the sin that separates you from Him. If you will allow God's influence to bring this truth to light, and if you allow Him to alter the way you see the sin, God *will* change your mind about it. You will be able to see the ugly truth of sin as He sees it, and your desire for it will fade away. You will not want sin anymore because it will no longer hold any value to you. And as this agreement with the perception of God grows within you, you will find a new life, because God is actually changing your heart. This life-change in heart and mind is called – repentance.

As long as you want to drink, do drugs, and live out-of-control – God will let you. As long as you want to lust, lie, and be offended – God will let you. And as long as you want to reject the truth spelled out for you by inventing some other way to be right in your own eyes – God will let you. But the fact is: As long as you want *you*, you don't really want God. If, on the other hand, you want to be set free – saved from you – you will need to respond to the voice of God and let Him change your 'want to.' You must let God change your mind and grant you repentance. Only then will you come to the end of yourself. Only then will you become nothing in your own eyes. Only then will you know the truth – and that truth set you free.

But once again, this change will not happen if you persist in dishonesty. You will need to seek with *all* your heart, talking to God about everything. Hebrews 4:16 encourages us to "draw near with confidence to the throne of grace." The word "confidence" is defined as a freedom or frankness in speaking, speaking *all* that one thinks.[1] And that is precisely the heart you should have – one that is open and willing to tell God exactly what you think: good or bad, right or wrong. Then that open heart must be willing to trust whatever God speaks to you in response. God sees everything laid bare before Him anyway (Hebrews 4:13), so why not go ahead and develop a real relationship with Him in which you are honest about the truth of your heart?

As you open up your life to Him with complete frankness, converse with God about everything that comes up. Do you want to be free from the fruit of [insert appropriate sin here]? Then look at it, talk to God about it, ask Him why you see it the way you do. Ask God how He sees it. Look deeper – past the apparent, past the obvious and find out your motive. Find the 'why.' Why do you like it? Why do you choose to value it? Don't just follow your shallow rules that say it is bad – find out why. Go to the source. Get to the root.

To help you understand this concept a little deeper, I would like to use an illustration of a bad fruit tree. Let's consider the fruit on the tree as your outward sin actions. As you look at your tree you will see many separate sins, the fruit of the flesh manifesting all over the branches. What most people try to do first is remove the bad fruit on their own, relying on their own understanding. After all, the fruit is sin, right? So why not just cut off that activity? Well, what happens when a gardener prunes back a fruit tree? It bears *more* fruit. One sin action not based on the voice of God cannot be removed by another sin action not based on the voice of God. See? Trying in your own labor to deliver yourself – save yourself from sin – will just add new self-produced sin fruit to the branch. Why "add sin to sin" (Isaiah 30:1)? What value is it to remove one crop of wickedness only to make room for the next? The fruit *will* return. Since Jesus said that a bad tree cannot bear good fruit (Matthew 7:18), you will need to perceive deeper to find God's remedy – the tree must die.

So, let's look at one individual bad fruit. On the surface, it has the *appearance* of being good. Like the fruit of original sin in the Garden of Eden, it may even be "delightful to the eyes" or "desirable to make one wise" (Genesis 3:6). If you will get honest, the truth is it looks good to you. You have believed the lie. Though you may tell yourself you shouldn't be this way – this is the way you are. Talk to God about this reality of your heart – He knows everything anyway. Why not go there in relationship with Him? Learn to develop this relationship as you honestly confess to Him the truth of your heart.

Next, gaze past the shiny surface of the sinful fruit in your life. Ask God to open your eyes and remove the tainted perception you were born with. Learn to look beneath the attractive surface – past the apparent, past the pretty – and see the rotted, worm-infested meat of the fruit for what it really is. Usually, the negative side of sin is not too difficult to perceive. What may be difficult, however, is to understand why we still desire it. And that is the question I hope you will become skilled in asking God: Why? Why do I do what I do? Where does this desire stem from? What causes it to grow, to manifest? Find and trust the truth God reveals to you. If you will believe Him, when you "draw near to God, He will draw near to you" (James 4:8).

As you look past the fruit of [insert appropriate sin here] you will see a branch supporting it, giving it life. This is the branch of value. Come to grips fully with this reality: You give value to your sin. You believe it is good and worth the time and labor to produce. You love your sin because it is beneficial, profitable, or in some way advantageous to you. You love and value your sin because of what it does for you. Therefore you have determined that it is valuable enough to lose relationship with God over. Through this branch of value, you have chosen to give glory and weight to that which suits you. First, you have given life to the bad fruit, and then – acting like God – you have called what *you* have created . . . 'good.' But you are not God.

Now let's follow the branch down further, past value to the trunk that supports it. Why value a heart that separates you from God? What motive causes you to assign value to the fruit of your sin? Well, because it gives *you* value. The trunk that supports all the other branches is *you* wanting to appear good and valuable in your own eyes. You want to see yourself as a person who has and does things that people around you call 'good.' You want to be admired and to garner validation for your life. You want to perceive personal worth within yourself and are willing to shape your life in order to become that person. You want to see yourself the way you choose – not sinful and base – but good and wise and valuable. And so you live your life crying out to the world, "Look at me, I have value!" But Jesus said, "No one is good except God alone" (Luke 18:19).

So why does your heart produce such a faulty perception? To know the truth, you must be willing to peer beneath the surface and see the gnarled and tangled tap root of self buried deep within. Will you see the tainted infection of Lucifer within your own heart: your character contaminated by the attitude of self-importance, your motive polluted by the deceptive influence of ego, and your best intention corrupted by the poison of opinion? This root of self is the source of sin which proclaims – at the earliest age – I have the right! I can choose my own path! I can determine what is right and wrong for me! I will call what I create good if I want to! I will assign value and glory to anything

I choose! I can and I will because . . . I AM! I Am My Own God! And while this underlying throne of self holds its fierce grip on your heart, mind, and soul – your life bears the fruit generated by the entrenched root. You believed the lie – as did we all.

So the tree must die. But will you be able to kill it on your own? Can a defiled heart filled with deception, corruption, and ego actually come up with a way to kill itself? No, though many have attempted to do just that. From contaminated hearts men have produced religions, denominations, and cults. With infected understanding they have shaped belief systems, creeds, and liturgies. And from faulty motives they have fashioned formulas, self-help psychology, and step-by-step programs. Then they prop it all up and buff the surface to a high sheen. The result? Polished slavery. The fruit they created – regardless of the motive – originated from the depraved root that still holds dominion over their souls. Everything done to close the gap between them and God only serves to widen the chasm. The tree of self lives.

In order to die to your self, you will need to listen to the Spirit who searches all things (I Corinthians 2:10). He will speak to you and show you the ugliness of your desire for *you*. If you will agree with His perception of your heart, the things that you give value to will change. With an ear to hear, the self-seeking woman who desires men *can be delivered*. With an ear to hear, the self-centered man who desires money and materialism *can be delivered*. And, with an ear to hear, the egotistical college student who is full of himself *can be delivered*. Even the average, everyday person who walks around convincing themselves that no one cares – with an ear given to God – *can be delivered*. A heart for God *can* replace your need for the house, the car, and the job that gives you value and makes you feel good about yourself. A heart for God *can* replace your obligation to ceremony and religious requirement used to justify yourself. And a heart for God *can* replace your need to pretend and to perform in order to gain the acceptance of men. The simple fact is that a heart for God *can* replace *you*. So ask God to grant you repentance from you.

When you let God change your perception, God will show you *real* value, and that is when you will realize there is none outside of Him. The song *Turn Your Eyes Upon Jesus* says it this way, ". . . and the things of the world will grow strangely dim in the light of His glory and grace." Your value in the things of this world, which include the value of your self, will fade compared to the weight and glory of God. But are you willing to become nothing? Are you willing to choose a perception that garners nothing for yourself? If you will allow God to change your mind about the reality of your heart, you will know the truth, and that truth – which came from the voice of God – will set you free from your inner self. That is how a bad tree is killed. That is deliverance. That is a salvation that is certain. You can choose to walk this path which costs you everything, or you can choose to stay right where you are – stuck and religiously spinning in circles to no avail. God grants you that choice.

I would like to leave you with a few verses that the Apostle Paul wrote to help make my last point. In order to be delivered from your sin and have new life, you must have a genuine relationship with Jesus – who sacrificed Himself for your sin – by becoming like Him in His death:

> *For if we have become united with Him in the*
> *likeness of His death, certainly we shall also be in*
> *the likeness of His resurrection . . .*
> *Romans 6:5*

To have new life, lay down every area of your heart just as Jesus did by saying, "Not my will, but Yours be done" (Luke 22:42). Your old self-will, self-understanding, and self-love must be put to death in order for God to remove your sin – the sin which chooses self over Him:

> *Knowing this, that our old self was crucified with*
> *Him, in order that our body of sin might be done*
> *away with, so we would no longer be slaves to sin.*
> *Romans 6:6*

This only happens if it happens. Don't religiously claim the death of Jesus like it was some vicarious magic show two thousand years ago. This must actually take place in your life. When it does, you will be saved from the sin that enslaves and controls you. The simple truth is:

He who has died is freed from sin.
Romans 6:7

Lastly, I encourage you to meditate on what God is speaking to you now. Don't leave anything to 'think so' or 'hope so' – instead *know so*. Talk to God honestly about how you see everything. Tell Him truthfully when you see sin in a good light or when deep down inside you like it. When you learn to see as He sees, you will be in agreement because you recognize reality for what it is. There will be no need for religious rules or pious games to make up for an unholy lifestyle. Imagine being set free from the pull of the flesh. The sinful nature *can* be nailed on the cross to wither away. If you will hold nothing back, you will be saved. Realize that only the bluntly honest dare to dig this deep, so beware the temptation to pull up short. Most of all, avoid leaning on your own misinformed understanding. Your guessing cannot deliver you. With all my heart, I encourage you to hear God and then trust His voice above everything else.

Endnotes

1. Spiros Zodhiates, TH.D., *The Complete Word Study Dictionary New Testament*, D/B/A AMG Publishers, copyright 1992 by Spiros Zodhiates and AMG International Inc. Zodhiates, page 1124, Greek #3954, *parresia*.

GLOSSARY

Definitions from:

James Strong, LL.D., S.T.D., *The New Strong's Exhaustive Concordance of the Bible*, Dictionary of the Greek Testament, copyright 1990 by Thomas Nelson Publishers.

James Strong, LL.D., S.T.D., *The New Strong's Exhaustive Concordance of the Bible*, Dictionary of the Hebrew Bible, copyright 1990 by Thomas Nelson Publishers.

Spiros Zodhiates, TH.D., *The Complete Word Study Dictionary New Testament*, D/B/A AMG Publishers, copyright 1992 by Spiros Zodhiates and AMG International Inc.

CHAPTER 1

Ancient: ". . . ask for the *ancient* paths" (Jeremiah 6:16). Concealed, i.e. the vanishing point; time out of mind. From the root word: to veil from site, i.e. to conceal (Strong's Hebrew #5769, #5956.)
WORKING DEFINITION: Ancient, concealed.

Concealed. Jeremiah urges us to ask for the ancient way to God. Though it is concealed, it can be found by those who are willing to search for it with all their hearts. There is no new, easy path that shortcuts a genuine heart change. Jesus said this road is narrow and difficult – few will find it.

Easy: "For My yoke is *easy* and My burden is light" (Matthew 11:30). Profitable, fit, good for any use (Zodhiates #5543.)
WORKING DEFINITION: Profitable.

Jesus' point was that compared to your natural yoke of slavery to self, His yoke is profitable and valuable. Only under the yoke of Christ will you be able to plow up your fallow ground and bear fruit for the Kingdom of God.

Repent: Repent, change the mind, relent. From two root words: denoting change of place or condition, and to exercise the mind, think, comprehend (Zodhiates #3340, #3326, #3539.)
WORKING DEFINITION: Change.

To change the mind is to let go of your old perception, your old understanding – and then choose the new insight God is revealing to you. What the heart chooses, the mind obeys. And when God truly changes your mind – your thoughts, motives, and actions will follow.

CHAPTER 2

Truth: Truth, reality; the unveiled reality lying at the basis of and agreeing with an appearance; the manifested, the veritable essence of matter (Zodhiates #225.)
WORKING DEFINITION: Unveiled reality.

There is only one God, therefore, there is only one truth. And it is this one truth that God speaks to you, unveiling the reality of all things. Everyone who is of this truth, hears His voice (John 18:37) – those who are not of this truth, exchange the truth of God for a lie (Romans 1:25).

Eye: "The *eye* is the lamp of the body . . ." (Matthew 6:22). To see, perceive with the eyes, to look at, implying not only the mere act of seeing but also the actual perception of what one sees (Zodhiates #3788, #3700.)
WORKING DEFINITION: Perception.

Your eye is your personal perception. Good or bad, this is the way you choose to perceive yourself, others, and the world around you. Few are willing to forsake their perception for the truth of God.

Clear: ". . . if your eye is *clear*, your whole body will be full of light" (Matthew 6:22). Single, i.e. not complex, easy, used of the

eye as not seeing double as when it is diseased. When the eye accomplishes its purpose of seeing things as they are, then it is single, healthy, perfect. Singleness, simplicity, absence of folds (Zodhiates #573.)
WORKING DEFINITION: Single.

Since all are born with the disease of sin blurring the eyes of their heart, healing is needed in order to have a clear perception. Only after God changes our double-vision will we be able to see reality and know the truth for what it really is.

Bad: "But if your eye is *bad*, your whole body will be full of darkness" (Matthew 6:23). Evil in a moral or spiritual sense, wicked, malicious, mischievous. From the root word: travail, toil, pain. It is labor which demands the whole strength of man (Zodhiates #4190, #4192.)
WORKING DEFINITION: Wicked from laboring in the strength of man.

According to the Greek definition, that which is bad is evil. It is evil because it roots from the labor of man. No matter how 'good' you want your perception to be, if it comes from your own understanding, *you* have created it. It is from your own labor, and thus it is evil.

Stumble: To cause to stumble, fall, to offend. From the root word: the trigger of a trap on which the bait is placed, and which, when touched by the animal, springs and causes it to close causing entrapment. *Skandalon* always denotes an enticement to conduct which leads to ruin (Zodhiates #4624, #4625.)
WORKING DEFINITION: Offend.

Although in contemporary society offense is often blamed on the offending party, offense is actually a chosen course of conduct by the person who is offended. It is the offended person who decides selfishly to garner value for himself by taking the sin-separating bait of self-justification. (Jesus offended many in John 6:52-66.)

See: "In a little while you will *see* me no more . . ." (John 16:16). To gaze, to look with interest and for a purpose, usually indicating the careful observation of details (Zodhiates #2334); to be a spectator of (Strong's Greek #2334.)
WORKING DEFINITION: Spectate.

See: ". . . and then after a little while you will *see* me" (John 16:16). To see, to perceive with the eyes, to look at, implying not only the mere act of seeing but also the actual perception of what one sees (Zodhiates #3700.)
WORKING DEFINITION: Perceive.

Of what value is it to be a simple spectator who merely observes but never perceives? All the careful observation in the world is useless without the understanding that only God can give.

CHAPTER 3

Believe: To believe, have faith in, to trust (Zodhiates #4100.)
WORKING DEFINITION: Trust.

To truly believe is to trust God. A genuine trust completely relies upon God, having full confidence that what He says is true. When you trust what God speaks to you, know that He is solid and steadfast. What God reveals will not only stand trustworthy today, but will stand the test of time. God can be trusted.

Seek: ". . . He is a rewarder of those who *seek* Him" (Hebrews 11:6). To seek out, search diligently for anything lost (Zodhiates #1567.)
WORKING DEFINITION: Search diligently.

You have as much of God as you desire. So, how much do you really want God? Those who seek, search, and cry out for God – find God. If you are willing to seek Him with all your heart you will be rewarded. Will you be diligent?

CHAPTER 4

Grace: "For by *grace* you have been saved through faith . . ." (Ephesians 2:8). Graciousness, of a manner or act, the divine influence upon the heart, and its reflection in the life, including gratitude (Strong's Greek #5485.)
WORKING DEFINITION: God's changing influence.

The benefit of God's grace influence – salvation – is conditional on trust (Ephesians 2:8). When trusted, His changing influence causes transformation. It affects the very heart of a man, delivering him from a life of self-bondage. God makes this life-changing influence available to all, but only those who are changed by it will be saved. (See Titus 2:11-12 for the definition of grace as found in the Scriptures.)

Instructing: "For the grace of God has appeared, bringing salvation to all men, *instructing* us to deny ungodliness and worldly desires . . ." (Titus 2:11-12). Originally to bring up a child, to educate, used of activity directed toward the moral and spiritual nurture and training of the child, to influence conscious will and action. To instruct, particularly a child or youth (Zodhiates #3811.)
WORKING DEFINITION: Training the will and action.

As God speaks to us, His grace is instructing us how to be righteous. To be made right with God we must accept the influence that trains us to say no to the ungodliness in our lives. The person who is delivered by God's instructing grace lets go of worldly desires rather than just excusing them or explaining them away.

Mercy: Mercy, compassion. To show compassion (Zodhiates #1653, #1656.)
WORKING DEFINITION: Compassion.

Only God is truly compassionate, and He shows mercy on whomever He pleases. Unlike grace, the compassion of mercy can affect the life without the condition of faith. Because of His compassion, God paid the penalty for sin by dying on the cross. Because of His compassion, He rose again – proving that death could not hold Him. And because of His compassion, we can know the mercy of the cross when we are willing to know the changing grace of that same cross.

Gospel: Originally a reward for good news, later becoming good news (Zodhiates #2098.)
WORKING DEFINITION: Good news.

The good news is more than just a story about Jesus. The good news is also more than just a religious concept passed on from one generation to another. The good news is: God has made a way for you to be delivered from the dominion of sin and self. You don't have to stay the same anymore. You can be set free from daily sin if you will let Jesus apply the cross to your life.

Vain: ". . . we also urge you not to receive the grace of God in *vain*" (II Corinthians 6:1). Empty, hollow (Zodhiates #2756.)
WORKING DEFINITION: Empty, hollow.

To receive God's changing influence in vain is to treat the things He says as if they were hollow and void of value. God is not empty. He is full of what is good, and right, and valuable. To treat His influence on you as a light thing is to discredit the God of the Universe Himself.

CHAPTER 5

Faith: Faith. Firm persuasion, conviction, belief in the truth, veracity, reality or faithfulness (Zodhiates #4102.)
WORKING DEFINITION: Trust.

Faith is being persuaded by the spoken voice of God (Romans 10:17). Most, however, are persuaded by the opinions of men passed on from one generation to the next. But the only way to have genuine faith is to get it from the mouth of God Himself. *Then* you will be persuaded and truly believe the truth that others only pretend to know.

Word: *(Rhema)* That which is spoken, a statement, word. Particularly a word as uttered by a living voice (Zodhiates #4487.)
WORKING DEFINITION: A word spoken by a living voice.

God speaks. Though there are many voices that clamor for attention, only one voice leads mankind to salvation. And it is only through hearing His voice that we obtain the faith required to gain that deliverance (Romans 10:17, Ephesians 2:8).

Scriptures: Used in the plural in the New Testament for the Holy Scriptures. From the root word: to engrave, to write (Zodhiates #1124, #1125.)
WORKING DEFINITION: Holy writings, the Bible.

The Bible, inspired by God, was written down by men who followed His voice. The purpose of the Scriptures is found within its pages: to show us that our sin is utterly sinful (Romans 7:13), to point us to Jesus (John 5:39-40), and to teach, reprove, correct, and train (II Timothy 3:16). As was true in Jesus' day, most religious people today choose to use it as a rule book rather than a tool to hear God and find a real delivered life in Christ.

Word: *(Logos)* Intelligence, word as the expression of that intelligence, discourse, saying, thing. Word, both the act of speaking and the thing spoken. Word as uttered by a living voice, a speaking, speech, utterance. From the root word: to speak intelligently (Zodhiates #3056, #3004.)

WORKING DEFINITION: A word spoken by a living voice.

God spoke to Adam. God spoke to Abraham, Isaac, and Jacob. God spoke to Moses and the prophets. God spoke to Peter, James, and John. When God came to this earth as Jesus, John called Him the Word/Logos because Jesus was the incarnate voice of God who speaks to all men. God will speak to you too, if you will have ears to hear.

Sin: Sin, missing the true end and scope of our lives, which is God. An offense in relation to God with emphasis on guilt. From the root word: to sin, miss a mark on the way, not to hit the mark. To err, swerve from the truth, go wrong (Zodhiates #266, #264.)

WORKING DEFINITION: Choosing to swerve from God.

Through Adam, sin gained dominion over mankind. Thus, from birth you have believed and acted according to your own selfish desires – and all this separated from God. The only way to be delivered from this wicked dominion is to be changed by the grace influence of God. God paid the penalty for sin on the cross, but it will be of no value to you unless you repent by taking your own cross and dying to the sin that controls you. Let go of your self and seize God.

CHAPTER 6

Evil: "And do not lead us into temptation, but deliver us from *evil*" (Matthew 6:13). Travail, toil, pain. It is labor which demands the whole strength of man (Zodhiates #4192.)

WORKING DEFINITION: Labor in the strength of man.

Jesus instructed us to pray for deliverance from our labor – from the strength we find in ourselves. We need to be set free from the efforts to be right in our own eyes, rescued from the excuses used to justify our undelivered sin, and saved from the need to boast in our strength rather than in our weakness. The chains of self-preservation and self-justification can be broken, but you cannot do it on your own – you need God. Ask Him to deliver you so you can know what it is to rely on Him rather than the strength of your own understanding.

CHAPTER 7

Calculate: "For which one of you, when he wants to build a tower, does not first sit down and *calculate* the cost to see if he has enough to complete it?" (Luke 14:29). To reckon, compute, calculate, figure out. From the root word: a small stone or pebble, a vote, suffrage, voice (Zodhiates #5585, #5586).
WORKING DEFINITION: Count, decide.

Cost is a paradox. Though you will never be able to work and earn a delivered relationship with God, the conditions required to know Him will cost you everything. Are you willing to surrender your heart, your mind, and your soul? Are you willing to relinquish your right to decide, your self-initiated actions, and your plans for the future? Are you willing to surrender your love for this world, your love for self, and your love for life? Your choices are your vote. And every time you cast your vote, God knows when you choose your own voice over His.

Factions: "I hear that divisions exist among you; and in part I believe it. For there must also be *factions* among you, so that those who are approved may become evident" (I Corinthians 11:18-19). Heresy, a form of religious worship, discipline, or opinion (Zodhiates #139); A choice, a party, or disunion (Strong's Greek #139.)
WORKING DEFINITION: A chosen side.

Everyone chooses a side. The majority of this world gives weight to the ideas and concepts of men. But there are a few who are willing to give weight to the voice of God alone. One person suppresses the truth, the other maintains it. And God sets apart the latter.

CHAPTER 8

Lucifer: The Morning Star (Strong's Hebrew #1966.)

After Lucifer fell, he was given the name Satan. In Greek, the name Satan means adversary (Zodhiates #4567) which is transliterated from the Hebrew word to attack, accuse (Strong's Hebrew #7854, #7853.) It is Satan's fallen nature to attack the truth and accuse any who would stand against his propaganda. He is crafty in his use of the spiritually blind to spread his unsubstantiated half-truths in order to deceive. If the world is Satan's backyard, then the false church is his playground.

Salvation: Safety, deliverance, preservation from danger or destruction (Zodhiates #4991.)
WORKING DEFINITION: Deliverance.

The salvation offered in the false church today is nothing more than a bad fire insurance policy that won't pay off in the end. Rather than finding the practical deliverance secured in taking the cross of Christ as their own, many settle for a religious charade that does not rescue them from the influence of selfish desire. Void of accountability, counterfeit believers find their security in the doctrine of a false, deficient gospel.

Saved: [Past tense of] To save, deliver, make whole, preserve safe from danger, loss, destruction (Zodhiates #4982.)
WORKING DEFINITION: Delivered.

To be saved is to be delivered. It is more than just being pardoned yet being left in bondage. When God truly saves a man, his chains are broken and left to rust on the floor. The sinful, self-centered control and manipulation of his life is then replaced by the guiding and instructing hand of God. Jesus, who was God in the flesh, did not die and rise again just to leave you half-saved, forced to excuse your sin away. You can be delivered. Ask Jesus to cleanse you from ALL of your sin and trust His voice completely. (In the NIV, I John 3:6 says, "No one who continues to sin has either seen him or known him" and in the NASB Updated it reads, "no one who sins has seen Him or knows Him.")

Free gift: "The wages of sin is death, but the *free gift* of God is eternal life. . ." (Romans 6:23). *Charisma* (#5486), from the root word: grace, which is the divine influence upon the heart, and its reflection in the life (Strong's Greek #5485), and the suffix *–ma*, indicating the result of grace (Zodhiates #5486.)
WORKING DEFINITION: Result of God's changing influence.

Though God extends the offer of eternal life to everyone freely, it is not without required conditions. Here are some of the Scriptural conditions: changing grace (Ephesians 2:8), faith (Ephesians 2:8), hearing God (Romans 10:17, John 10:27), repent and prove that repentance by deeds (Acts 26:20, Matthew 3:8), cessation of sin (II Timothy 2:19, I John 3:6), life application of the cross (Matthew 10:38, Luke 9:23), and Jesus Himself said you must count the cost (Luke 14:28-33) and that you must love God with all your heart, soul, mind, and strength (Matthew 22:35). Therefore, the inaccurate translation of "free gift" is an unfortunate deception of the passage. Eternal life is the *result* of God's changing influence.

Forgive: [Various words] To let loose, unbind (Zodhiates #630); to send forth or away, let go from oneself (Zodhiates #863); remission, the putting away of sin and deliverance from the power of sin (Zodhiates #859); to grant favor (Strong's Greek

#5483), which is from the root word: grace, the divine influence upon the heart, and its reflection in the life (Strong's Greek #5485.)
WORKING DEFINITION: Remove.

To be forgiven is to actually have your sin removed. This doesn't mean you have never sinned before. Nor does it mean you will not sin again. But forgiveness is more than a cheap pardon that absolves you from guilt and accountability but then leaves your unrepentant tendency to sin intact. When God forgives, He changes you by removing the control and the pull of your flesh.

Power: "For the [spoken] word of the cross is to those who are perishing foolishness, but to us who are being saved it is the *power* of God" (I Corinthians 1:18). Power, especially achieving power (Zodhiates #1411.)
WORKING DEFINITION: Achieving power.

The power of God is His ability to achieve anything He so desires. Therefore, there is no sin, no habit, and no power over your life that cannot be broken by the achieving power of God. If you are willing to carry your cross (Luke 9:23) and to be buried through a baptism of death (Romans 6:4), God has the ability to raise you to a new, delivered life. Ephesians 3:20 says that God "is able to do immeasurably more than all we ask or imagine, according to His [achieving] power that is at work within us" (NIV).

Fallen away: ". . . and then have *fallen away*, it is impossible to renew them again to repentance" (Hebrews 6:6). To fall aside or away, err, stray, lapse. Denoting a falling away, an abandonment . . . in every case signify[ing] deliberate acts of sin (Zodhiates #3895); to fall aside, to apostatize (Strong's Greek #3895.)
WORKING DEFINITION: Deliberate abandonment, apostasy.

The very fact that the word apostasy is in the Scriptures should remind true believers that "by standing firm you will gain life"

(Luke 21:19). Abandonment by apostasy is always an option for the truly delivered if they should choose to go back to a lifestyle of sin. If you are a believer, you should desire "to make your calling and election sure" (II Peter 1:10-11 NIV), to choose to continue (Colossians 1:23), remain (John 15:6 NIV), persevere (Hebrews 10:36 NIV), and be persistent (Roman 2:7 NIV) in order to avoid being entangled again (II Peter 2:20). When Ezekiel warned the religious of his day that a righteous man who turns away from his righteousness would be held accountable for his sin, they argued that "The way of the Lord is not right" (Ezekiel 18:24-25). God's response back was the crux of the matter: "Is My way not right? Is it not your ways that are not right?" (25).

Snatch: ". . . no one will *snatch* them out of My hand" (John 10:28). To seize upon with force, to rob (Zodhiates #726). WORKING DEFINITION: Rob by force.

Your relationship with God is a covenant between you and Him. Therefore, no outside force can pry open His hands and steal you away. No violent attempt by some nefarious principality is able to wrestle you out of His care. God is an attentive shepherd and ever capable to safeguard His sheep.

Abandon: "The Spirit clearly says that in later times some will *abandon* the faith" (I Timothy 4:1 NIV). To withdraw, remove oneself, forsake, desert, retire, cease from something (Zodhiates #868); to remove, instigate a revolt, to desist, desert (Strong's Greek #868.)
WORKING DEFINITION: Desert, cease the faith.

And what is it that I Timothy 4:1 says some will desert, revolt, withdraw, and cease from? From *the faith*. Not from a false faith, or some personal, half-hearted belief system labeled faith. Paul makes it very clear that the abandonment and desertion is away from THE faith – and there is only one (Ephesians 4:5). Now, a person is not labeled a deserter because he is the enemy camped outside the gate of the kingdom. No, a person is labeled a deserter after he has sworn allegiance and served the King and then determines the cost is too great and thus abandons his post. Simply stated, you cannot cease what you are not doing in the first place. You can choose to remove yourself from a relationship with God.

Irrevocable: ". . . for the gifts and calling of God are *irrevocable*" (Romans 11:29). Without repentance. From two words: -*a* without and to change one's mind, to regret (Zodhiates #278, #3338.)
WORKING DEFINITION: Without regret.

God does not regret the mercy He has shown the world. He does not regret dying on the cross to pay for our sin. And He in no way regrets extending grace to mankind to instruct them how to choose His influence over the influence of sin and self.

CHAPTER 9

Peter: ". . . you are *Peter* . . ." (Matthew 16:18). A piece of rock (Strong's #4074); a stone, a piece or fragment of a rock such as a man might throw (Zodhiates #4074.)
WORKING DEFINITION: Movable stone.

Rock: ". . . and upon this *rock* I will build My church" (Matthew 16:18). A mass of rock (Strong's Greek #4073); a projecting rock or cliff (Zodhiates #4073.)
WORKING DEFINITION: Big rock, immovable bedrock.

Jesus is the rock of our salvation – there is no questioning that. But the concept Jesus is teaching His disciples in Matthew 16 is that He will build His church on the revelation of who He is. God reveals Himself. This revelation is paramount not only for deliverance from daily sin, but also for developing a genuine relationship with Jesus.

Go: "*Go* therefore and make disciples of all the nations . . ." (Matthew 28:19). To transport oneself (Zodhiates #4198); to traverse, i.e. travel (Strong's Greek #4198.)
WORKING DEFINITION: As you are going.

Jesus never commanded his followers to go. He commanded them to make disciples. When the Greek is parsed correctly, His point was for them to make disciples *as they traveled.* This verse was never intended to be taken legalistically as a call to foreign soil. God intended for his followers to become disciplined by hearing where He says to go – and then to teach others how to be disciplined by God when they get there.

Make disciples: ". . . *make disciples* of all nations . . ." (Matthew 28:19). To make a disciple, to instruct with the purpose of making a disciple (Zodhiates #3100); to disciple (Strong's Greek #3100.)
WORKING DEFINITION: Make disciples

A disciple is a person disciplined by God. This is far more than just going through the motions in a Sunday school every week. A person disciplined by God hears, trusts, and obeys the Father with all his heart. To instruct another person in true discipleship can be both difficult and time consuming. The fruit, however, is worth it.

(*No definitions in Chapter 10)

CHAPTER 11

Hesitate: "How long will you *hesitate* between two opinions?" (I Kings 18:21). To hop, to skip over, to hesitate, to limp, to dance (Strong's Hebrew #6452.)
WORKING DEFINITION: Hesitate, dance.

If you hesitate between two opinions, don't sugarcoat it as some form of 'spiritual caution.' Either follow God or don't. There is no half-way Christianity, no matter what the religious say. And refusing to choose God by limping about won't garner you any sympathy.

Intended: "Therefore, I was not vacillating when I *intended* to do this, was I?" (II Corinthians 1:17). To resolve in council, to decree (Zodhiates #1011); to advise, deliberate, resolve (Strong's Greek #1011.)
WORKING DEFINITION: Resolved.

Be settled, be resolved. Find God's will and stand firmly on it. There should be no shifting of weight onto something else – something less stable or more comfortable. Have the kind of relationship with Christ that is willing to stand firm where He tells you regardless of the consequences.

Tossed: "But he must ask in faith without any doubting, for the one who doubts is like the surf of the sea, driven and *tossed* by the wind" (James 1:6). To stir up a fire by fanning it, to move to and fro, to toss, agitate as waves (Zodhiates #4494); to breeze up, to agitate (Strong's Greek #4494.)
WORKING DEFINITION: Agitate

The follower of God should be like a rock onto which the waves crash. Unflinching. Immovable. Resolute. This will only happen when you trust. Otherwise, you will be agitated by the things of God, with no hope of remedy to calm your soul. Trust God or be tossed.

CHAPTER 12

Perfect: "Therefore you are to be *perfect*, as your heavenly Father is *perfect*" (Matthew 5:48). Finished, that which has reached its end, term, limit; hence, complete, full, wanting in nothing (Zodhiates #5046.)

WORKING DEFINITION: Complete.

Most 'spiritual' leaders not only refuse to instruct how to become complete, but actually teach it away by excuse and blather. "I'm not perfect, just forgiven" isn't going to justify you before a holy God on that day. God is more than able to train you up completely. Have the heart that desires to change deeper each day, and you will become mature lacking in nothing.

APPENDIX

Confidence: ". . . draw near with *confidence* to the throne of grace" (Hebrews 4:16). Freedom or frankness in speaking; freedom in speaking all that one thinks or pleases (Zodhiates #3954.)
WORKING DEFINITION: Speak honestly.

God sees all, so talk honestly with Him. If you are hindered in speaking freely before God – ask Him to help you change. This is the only way you will ever come into complete agreement with God. It is His desire to transform you, so have the courage to speak up honestly, holding nothing back from Him.

INDEX OF SCRIPTURE REFERENCES

Genesis 17-22
Romans 4:3
Galatians 3:16
Galatians 3:17
Hebrews 11:6
Romans 10:17
Ephesians 2:8
Romans 10:17
Jeremiah 6:19
I Corinthians 2:14
John 5:39-40
II Timothy 3:16
I Corinthians 2:14
Matthew 4:4
Titus 1:3
John 17:17
Hebrews 4:12
John 10:27
John 10:5
Proverbs 4:7
Amos 4:13
Amos 3:7
Romans 14:23
John 12:48
Romans 1:17
Hebrews 4:2
Romans 4:20
I John 2:27
Ephesians 4:5

Ephesians 2:8-10
I John 2:6
I John 2:6
John 5:19
John 8:28
Philippians 2:6-8
John 12:49
John 14:31
Matthew 7:21-22
Luke 6:46
Titus 1:16
Mark 7:13
James 2:14-26
James 2:21-26
Genesis 22:12
Acts 26:20
Matthew 6:13
Matthew 16:24-27
II Corinthians 10:5
James 1:22-25
I Samuel 15:22
Hebrews 11:6
John 14:21
John 15:14
Luke 8:21
John 3:36
Colossians 2:21
Colossians 2:23
Jeremiah 31:33

CHAPTER 6

I John 2:6
James 1:17
John 6:28-29
Romans 7:18
John 15:5
Romans 1:5
Romans 14:23

CHAPTER 7

Luke 14:28-29
Matthew 13:44
Philippians 3:8
Luke 18:29-30
Matthew 7:14
Matthew 7:13
Jeremiah 6:16

Matthew 16:24
Romans 6:6
John 12:24
Luke 21:17
Acts 14:22
II Timothy 3:12
II Timothy 2:8-9
Roman 8:17
I Corinthians 11:18-19
John 16:2
Matthew 16:25
Luke 14:33
Matthew 5:10

CHAPTER 8

PART 1

Ephesians 2:8
II Corinthians 5:17
Isaiah 14:13-14
Revelation 12:4
Revelation 12:7
Revelation 12:8-9
Hebrews 2:7
Romans 5:12
John 14:6
Colossians 1:13
Matthew 7:13-14
I Corinthians 6:3
Ephesians 3:10-11
Hebrews 6:17
Ephesians 2:8
Titus 2:11-12
Romans 10:17
James 2:17
Acts 26:20
Matthew 4:4

PART II

I Peter 1:16
I John 3:9
Jeremiah 17:14
Acts 15:11
Ephesians 2:9
Romans 10:3
Acts 15:11
Romans 11:5
John 1:12-13
John 3:27
Matthew 22:1-14
John 13:18
Acts 4:12
Romans 8:16
Romans 6:23
Romans 6:23
Titus 2:11
Ephesians 2:8
James 2:20
Acts 10:43
II Timothy 2:25
Luke 24:47
Acts 15:9
I John 1:7
II Corinthians 5:17
II Timothy 2:19
II Corinthians 2:16
I Corinthians 1:18
Revelation 21:8
Psalms 119:81
Matthew 13:20-21
Proverbs 20:21
II Corinthians 13:5
II Timothy 3:15
Psalms 85:9
Isaiah 45:22
Psalms 119:94

PART III

I Corinthians 9:24
John 10:27
Luke 9:23
Titus 2:11
Titus 2:12
Acts 13:43
Romans 1:17
I John 3:7-8
I John 3:9
Acts 26:20
Matthew 4:4
I Peter 2:2
Ephesians 4:13
Jeremiah 4:3
Romans 8:29
Hebrews 4:15
James 1:14-15
I Corinthians 10:13
I John 2:1
Revelation 12:10
Job 1:11
Zechariah 3:1
John 10:27
Hebrews 4:15
Hebrews 12:6
Ephesians 4:27
Romans 6:1
Galatians 5:4
Galatians 5:1
Galatians 4:9

PART IV

Hebrews 11:15
Galatians 6:7-8
Proverbs 15:10
Proverbs 10:17

Proverbs 12:1
II Peter 2:20-21
Romans 11:20-22
John 15:2, 6
II Timothy 2:12
Hebrews 3:12
Hebrews 6:4-5
Hebrews 10:26
I Peter 3:18
Hebrews 10:27
Hebrews 6:7-8
Revelation 2:4-5
Revelation 2:16
Philippians 2:12
Acts 14:22
Hebrews 10:31
John 10:28
I Timothy 4:1
Romans 8:15-17
Romans 8:23, 25
Romans 11:29
Philippians 3:11-12
I Peter 1:5-6
Philippians 3:12-15
I Corinthians 9:26-27
Hebrews 10:36
Hebrews 12:1
Matthew 24:13

CHAPTER 9

Zechariah 9:16
Matthew 18:20
II Corinthians 6:18
Acts 4:32
Philippians 1:27
I John 3:10
Malachi 3:18
I Thessalonians 5:17

Romans 8:14
Romans 12:2
Matthew 16:17-18
I Peter 2:7-8
Matthew 16:18
I John 5:14-15
Psalms 66:18
Ephesians 5:8
Daniel 12:3
Isaiah 60:3
Matthew 28:19-20
Matthew 23:15
Colossians 1:18
John 15:16
Luke 14:33
Matthew 10:37
Luke 14:26
Hebrews 12:8
I John 2:19
Acts 15:1
I Corinthians 5:11
Titus 1:10, 16
Acts 26:20
Matthew 3:8
I Corinthians 5:11
Matthew 9:10-11
I Corinthians 11:27-29
Psalms 107:35
John 7:38
Romans 12:5
Romans 14:12
James 3:1
I John 4:1
Colossians 1:18
I Timothy 2:12
I Timothy 3:6
I Timothy 4:11
I Thessalonians 5:12
Ephesians 4:12-16

II Thessalonians 3:9
I Timothy 4:12
Titus 2:7
John 10:27
Hebrews 13:8
John 7:24
Romans 4:9
II Timothy 2:15
Matthew 4:4
I John 3:1
Zechariah 9:16
Ephesians 5:26-27
Philippians 2:15-16

CHAPTER 10

Isaiah 1:21
Jeremiah 18:12
Jeremiah 2:8
Jeremiah 3:3
Jeremiah 2:24
Ezekiel 16:15-16
Proverbs 7:16-17
Ezekiel 16:17
I Chronicles 5:25
II Timothy 4:3
Proverbs 7:11-12
Proverbs 7:7
Isaiah 30:1
Ezekiel 16:51-52
Jeremiah 3:4-5
Isaiah 1:21
Ezekiel 16:37
II Timothy 4:3-4
James 4:4
II Peter 2:19
Malachi 2:7
Mark 7:13
Job 33:14

Jeremiah 32:33
Isaiah 30:9-11
Isaiah 28:15
Isaiah 1:21
Ezekiel 7:20

CHAPTER 11

1 Kings 18:21
Matthew 7:22-23
Romans 10:2-3
Matthew 23:25-28
II Chronicles 25:2
Luke 12:1
I Corinthians 5:6
Ecclesiastes 5:5
Malachi 1:14
Hosea 10:4
II Corinthians 3:6
II Timothy 3:16
II Peter 1:20
Matthew 23:15
Matthew 7:1
John 7:24
I Corinthians 4:3-5
Mark 7:6-8
John 10:27
Galatians 4:29
I Kings 18:21
II Corinthians 1:17
James 1:6-8
II Peter 3:16
Titus 1:16
James 4:8
I Corinthians 15:58
Psalm 26:1

CHAPTER 12

II Chronicles 16:9
Jeremiah 6:16
Romans 8:5
John 6:63
II Chronicles 16:9
II Corinthians 12:9
Isaiah 66:2
Isaiah 30:18
Titus 2:12
Jeremiah 4:3
Matthew 13:23
I John 2:27
Jeremiah 6:10
Psalm 42:7
Jeremiah 22:13
Matthew 7:26-27
Psalm 127:1
Matthew 3:3
Isaiah 40:4
Hebrews 12:13
Luke 3:8
Acts 26:20
Deuteronomy 4:2
Romans 14:23
I Timothy 1:19
Isaiah 55:9
Matthew 5:48
Romans 8:29
Romans 11:36
Matthew 18:20
Isaiah 60:3
Luke 14:29
II Timothy 1:8
II Timothy 3:12
I Peter 4:1
I Peter 3:16
Luke 6:26
Matthew 10:22
John 15:18

Hebrews 12:2
Colossians 1:24
I Corinthians 4:10
II Corinthians 4:17
Revelation 2:10
Ephesians 6:12
Psalm 119:53
Numbers 25:6-13
Matthew 21:12
Ephesians 6:17
Hebrews 4:12
Jeremiah 6:10
Jeremiah 48:10
Luke 11:37-52
John 8:3-6
Matthew 26:63
John 1:23
Ephesians 4:15
Zechariah 4:10
I John 4:1
II Corinthians 13:5
II Timothy 2:15
Acts 17:11
Hebrews 11:38
Isaiah 61:4
Psalms 139

Matthew 12:34
John 8:32
John 17:17
Hebrews 4:16
Hebrews 4:13
Isaiah 30:1
Matthew 7:18
Genesis 3:6
James 4:8
Luke 18:19
I Corinthians 2:10
Romans 6:5
Luke 22:42
Romans 6:6
Romans 6:7

APPENDIX

Deuteronomy 4:29
Romans 3:4
I Corinthians 14:33
Acts 26:20
Ephesians 2:9
Colossians 2:20-21
Colossians 2:23
James 1:26
James 3:8

If you are interested in further studies by Remnant Ministries
visit
www.simplyreal.org

There you will find:

A study guide to *Asking for the Ancient Path*
Free downloadable music by Simply Real
Instructional Teach-Mails
and more . . .

And

Coming Soon
another book by Jeff S. Baron

After God's Own Heart

Hearing
Understanding the Voice of God
Applying